Eric

Thank you for being part of our "Yellow Dog Cafe" Team

Happy Cooking

Stuart J Bostom
10-22-2010

Yellow Dog Café Cookbook

Stuart Borton

© Copyright 2010 by Stuart Borton

All rights reserved.

No part of this book may be reproduced or transmitted in any form or by any means, electronic or mechanical, including photocopying, recording, or any other information storage and retrieval system, without the written permission of the publisher.

All inquiries should be addressed to:

Yellow Dog Printing, LLC
905 U. S. Highway 1
Malabar, Florida 32950

http://www.yellowdogcafe.com
Stuart@yellowdogcafe.com

321-953-3912

Mention of specific companies, organizations or authorities in this book does not imply endorsement by the publisher, nor does mention of specific companies, organizations, or authorities imply that they endorse this book. Printed by FUPITC for Yellow Dog Printing, LLC.

Book edited by Mia Crews

Cover design by Lesmarie Velez and Keith Betterley
Cover photo by Keith Betterley
Layout and design by Nancy Borton, Mia Crews and Lesmarie Velez
Food styling by Nancy Borton, Mia Crews and Lesmarie Velez

Photos by Keith Betterley, or as attributed; pet photos contributed by owners
Original dog artwork by Richard Courier

International Standard Book No. 978-0-9842916-0-1

Library of Congress Catalog Card No. 2010930957

Library of Congress Cataloging-in-Publication Data

Borton, Stuart
    Yellow Dog Cafe™ Cookbook / by Stuart Borton
First edition
        p.   cm.
Includes index.
ISBN 978-0-9842916-0-1 hardcover
1. Food–recipes. 2. Cookery–recipes. 1. Title.

This book is dedicated in loving memory
to Blanche, the Cafe's namesake.

Acknowledgements

I'd like to thank my wife, Nancy Tinio Borton, for her inspiration,
encouragement, her keen eye for design and layout of the book
and help with many of her family recipes;
my mother and father, Jean and Jake Borton;
Nancy's mom and dad, Nancy and Salvatore Tinio;
my editor Mia Crews for all the help and guidance in putting this book together;
and special thanks to our entire team at the Cafe:
David Ness, General Manager & Alberto Sierra, Executive Chef
Billy Rose, Justine Schmidt, Miles Matthews,
Ranebeaux Randall, Mike Marrero, Paul Modungo, Tim Coyle, Susan Hartgrave,
Lesmarie Velez, Cathy Mussman, Steve Snarey, Wendy Miller, Danny Stala,
Anisia Desoto, Sean Alsobrook, Michelle Dezman, Eric Garloch, Meridith Sykes,
Laurel Rothschild, Monique Hicks, Summer Mckee, Bill Mintz, Richard Quinn, Carlos Soto,
Regina Acquaviva, Joliz Tavarez, John Blanca.
Thank you to our proofreaders:
Maureen Okerstrom, Carol Nepi, Rebecca Wood, Michele Black and Sheila Lowenstein
Many thanks to Mort and Sheila Lowenstein for their inspired marketing concept for the Café
and also for giving Blanche a great home!
Special thanks to my friend Victor Doherty, for all his years of dedication;
also deserving my appreciation are chefs I have worked with in the past
and learned so much from, to name a few: Eleanor Miles, Lela Coyer, Jurgen Starckjohann,
Ben Bishop, Jason Beter and Bill Middelton.

I'd also like to acknowledge *In Touch Magazine*, *SpaceCoast Living Magazine*,
Florida Today, *Vero Beach Press Journal*, *Central Florida News 13*,
Orlando Sentinel, *Florida Travel + Leisure*, *32963 Magazine* and *Aldia Today*
for their support of Yellow Dog Café™ over the years.

CONTENTS

Stuart Borton	10
Nancy Borton	12
Yellow Dog Café Photos	13
Products	20
Introduction	22
Staff Photos	23
The Prepared Cook	24
Creating Your Own Spice Mixes	25
Sauces and Gravies	30
Breads & Batters	44
Eggs	58
Grits	70
Soups	74
Salads	86
Sandwiches	92
Sides	100
Appetizers	110
Entrees	136
Desserts	154
Homemade Dog Food	200
We Love Cats, Too!	203
Glossary of Cooking Terms	204
Weights & Measures	211
Yellow Dog Artwork	212
Index	213

SPECIAL DINING EDITION

spacecoast

TOP CHEFS SHARE THEIR SIGNATURE DISHES

Nancy and Stuart Borton of the Yellow Dog Café

BON APPÉTIT BREVARD

FINE DINING BEST LOCAL RESTAURANT

LOCAL FAVORITES
DISTINCT AREA TASTES & PLACES

MARCH 2009

Photo by John Sluter

The Bortons at Stuart's Bistro, 1993.

Stuart Borton

Stuart Borton is chef and co-owner of Yellow Dog Café in Malabar, Florida. He and his wife Nancy opened the Yellow Dog Café in February 1997. Specializing in "comfort food with a flair," Yellow Dog Café is renowned for its excellent service, impeccable cuisine and riverfront views. Yellow Dog Café was recently named one of Brevard County's best local fine dining restaurants by *Space Coast Living* magazine. *Florida Travel and Life* magazine featured Yellow Dog Café as one of the best tables with a view in the state of Florida. I*n Touch Magazine* recently wrote about Yellow Dog Café: "A legendary Florida restaurant cooks up one of the world's best chicken dishes." *Orlando Sentinel* food reviewer Scott Joseph wrote that the Yellow Dog Café is "adrift in flavors along the river's edge; The views of the Indian River make Yellow Dog Café a scenic setting for a wonderful dining excursion."

Stuart is originally from Michigan and credits his mom Jean for his culinary beginnings. After a stint in the Army when he was stationed in Germany, he traveled to Japan and Australia where he settled in Adelaide to work in the insurance industry. Soon he purchased his first restaurant in the city's old Parliament building. As luck would have it, the government legalized gambling in southern Australia, and the train station across the street from Stuart's restaurant became a casino. Crowds waiting to get into the casino found Stuart's establishment and turned it into a roaring success. Later, Stuart opened another restaurant in Adelaide called Oxfords Cafe, which became a popular hangout specializing in desserts for the after-theater crowd.

While vacationing back in the United States, Stuart met Nancy in Orlando, Florida. After a whirlwind romance, Stuart moved back to America, married Nancy and opened a restaurant in St. Louis, Michigan, at the Michigan Livestock Exchange. They named it The Steer Inn, specializing in steaks. The cold weather, however, left the couple missing Florida. In short order, they moved to the Micco area where they opened two restaurants, Stuart's Bistro and The Pizza Store.

For years, Stuart and Nancy dreamed of owning a restaurant on the water. Discovering an old building on the Indian River Lagoon in Malabar, they quickly purchased and remodeled it in 1997. Their dream became a reality when they opened the Yellow Dog Café on February 13, 1998. Over the years, the Bortons have added a riverfront covered porch and a dock on the beach with a landscaped area for weddings and special occasions. Guests are welcome to stroll along the river and walk the pier before and after dinner. The porch is also the perfect place to enjoy an afternoon cocktail, appetizer or simply coffee and dessert.

Jean Borton

Stuart is active in the Brevard County community. He is the Chair Elect for the Greater Palm Bay Chamber of Commerce and Vice President for Restaurants for the Space Coast Chapter of the Florida Restaurant and Lodging Association.

Stuart also participates on the Citizen Advisory Council for the St. Johns River Water Management District, and he was recently appointed to the Brevard County Culinary Advisory Committee. Stuart also teaches a children's cooking class at a local elementary school.

Nancy Tinio Borton

My wife Nancy, my inspiration, was named after her mother Nancy who owned and operated Tinio's Pizzeria in Mendon, Massachusetts. Nancy was inspired and motivated by her mother's passion for the hospitality industry. Nancy's mom came from Italy as a young girl and met her future husband Salvatore Tinio in Massachusetts shortly after she arrived. The Tinio family says that young Nancy was born under a restaurant table, learning to cook and conduct a successful culinary business at her mother's feet.

At age 12, Nancy got her first job working at Lake Nipmuc where she served assorted treats to the beach crowd. Soon after, she worked at a grocery store kiosk which she was managing by the age of 13. Discovering early on that she had a talent and passion for the food industry, she enrolled in the Worcester Fanning Trade School where she graduated with a degree in restaurant business administration. She won several competitions for cake decorating and was class president in her senior year.

Shortly after graduation, she was hired by the Abody family to manage The El Morocco Restaurant in Worcester, Massachusetts. Working for a large family operation quickly taught Nancy diplomacy and poise under pressure. She is the most intuitive and perceptive person I know.

Anyone who knows Nancy can't help but be inspired by her attention to detail, from how the food tastes, looks and is presented. And it doesn't stop there; she takes responsibility for the eclectic decor of the restaurant and is highly skilled at staff management, which is so important in the restaurant business.

Nancy's talent doesn't just extend to decorating and food. She coined the philosophy of our cooking style at the Yellow Dog Café™ with a single phrase: ***"comfort food with a flair."*** Customers at The Dog can enjoy comfort food with a flair, surrounded by Nancy's cozy collections of dog memorabilia, marionettes, and Yellow Dog artwork.

Nancy Borton

Nancy Tinio

Yellow Dog Café
905 Highway U.S. 1
Malabar, Florida on the Indian River Lagoon

Stuart Borton, forefront, and Executive Chef Alberto Sierra

INDULGENCES

Where the celebs dine

A legendary Florida restaurant cooks up one of the world's best chicken dishes

Stuart Borton, chef of The Yellow Dog Café, boasts that it's the perfect combination of juices that makes his chicken a mouth-watering sensation. Borton enjoys the challenge of taking an existing dish and improving upon it. When a chef he hired showed him how to make an onion-crusted chicken dish, he adapted the recipe and made it his own. "That's what you do when you're self-taught. You copy what someone else has done and learn," says the culinary expert, who co-owns The Yellow Dog Café in Malibar, Fla. with his wife Nancy.

Recounting his introduction to the onion-crusted chicken, Borton notes, "The chef's sauce was made from ketchup, sugar and bacon." Borton created a new sauce using caramelized sugar and a combination of citrus juices.

Celebrities who have visited The Yellow Dog include *America's Most Wanted*'s host John Walsh, singer Arlo Guthrie and *General Hospital*'s Wally Kurth. When Florida Governor Jeb Bush celebrated his 49th birthday at the restaurant last February, Borton presented him with a cake in the shape of the American flag.

Chef Borton started his first restaurant in Australia, then moved to America and opened the Yellow Dog in 1998.

President Bush's brother Jeb's birthday cake was red, white and blue.

John Walsh sampled the "comfort food with a flair."

The restaurant has charming river views.

One of the house specialities: dogbone brownies!

Onion–Crusted Chicken with Caramel Citrus Glaze
Makes 2 servings

- 1/4 cup vegetable oil
- 1 lb. boneless chicken breast halves, pounded to 1/4-inch thick
- Salt and pepper
- 1 egg, beaten
- Crusted Onions (see recipe below)
- Caramel Citrus Glaze (see recipe below)

In nonstick skillet, heat oil. Season chicken breasts with salt and pepper. Dip chicken into beaten egg, then into crusted onions. Place chicken in skillet. Cook 10 min., turning once or until golden and cooked through. Spoon glaze over chicken. Serve over mashed potatoes, if desired.

Work time: 10 min. Total time: 30 min., plus crusted onions and sauce prep time

Crusted Onions
Makes 2 servings

- 1 large red onion, peeled and sliced
- 1 cup milk
- 2 cups flour
- 1/4 tsp. cayenne pepper
- 1/4 tsp. pepper
- 1 cup vegetable oil

In large bowl, place onions in milk. In another bowl, combine flour, cayenne and pepper. In nonstick skillet, heat oil. In small batches, dredge milk-coated onion in the flour mixture. Place in skillet, fry 5 min., or until crispy. Remove and place in plate lined with paper towel (to blot excess grease); cool completely. Finely chop fried onions.

Chef's tip: For a shortcut use canned French Fried Onions

Caramel Citrus Glaze
Makes 2 servings

- 4 strips bacon, finely chopped
- 1 red onion, peeled and finely chopped
- 2 cups sugar
- 2 cups water
- 1 Tbs. tomato purée
- 1 each orange, lemon and lime, juiced

In nonstick skillet, cook bacon and onion 5 min., or until onion is translucent. Add sugar, water and tomato purée. Reduce mixture until thick. Add citrus juices.

Cooking secret: Secret to juicy, tender chicken: Don't pound too thin, and cook slowly.

Chef Borton, who loves a challenge, discovered a classic dish that brings in the crowds.

Aussie

Winston

Winston

This is Nancy and Stuart's family of pets: their cats Winston and Aussie, their adopted dog Easy and Aussie's friend, Benson the Bird, who likes to go along for the ride.

Easy

Aussie and Benson

Yellow Dog Products

To purchase shirts, hats, house vinaigrettes, wine glasses or more copies of this cookbook, visit the Café at 905 U.S. Highway 1 Malabar, Florida

Call 321-956-3334 or check out our web site www.yellowdogcafe.com

Introduction

For many years people have been asking me for recipes. I wrote this book for them as a way for me to share my bag of tricks. For most of my adult life, I've worked in the kitchen and have learned many shortcuts. This is my opportunity to pass them on to you.

The best advice I can give you is to start out by being a prepared cook. I believe that a good arsenal of sauces, marinades, rubs and a bit of organization will take even a seasoned cook to a higher level.

Being prepared takes a lot of pressure off when you arrive in your kitchen to start a meal. Having a spice mix or sauce made ahead can save you a lot of time and makes meal preparation a smooth and stress free event. Being a prepared cook allows you to bring everything together easily at the last minute for a perfectly timed and well executed meal.

Whether you are preparing meals for a restaurant or for your family at home, planning and organization are key. At Yellow Dog Café, we start off our day with what the French call "mise en place," meaning to have all necessary ingredients for a dish prepared and ready to combine, up to the point of cooking. Our staff takes daily stock of appropriate spice mixes, sauces, soups, batters and glazes ready to enhance and accompany not only standard menu items but also daily specials.

We also vary the menu according to seasons, taking advantage of fresh fruits and vegetables available at different times of the year. Hot soups and hearty breads for winter, fresh greens in spring, cold salads in summer and pumpkin or squash in the fall. Try growing your favorite herbs in your own garden, or if limited by space, in a kitchen window using the herbs fresh or drying them for later use.

I have provided recipes to make spice mixes, sauces, dressings and glazes that will take the simplest meal to new heights or make the most complicated meal easier to prepare.

Stuart Borton

"Every dog has a bag of tricks. Here's mine!" ~ Stuart

THE PREPARED COOK

Creating Your Own Spice Mixes

Stuart's House Spice Mix

Makes 2½ cups

Ingredients

¼	cup dried rosemary
½	cup garlic powder
1	cup dried parsley
¼	cup dried oregano
¼	cup dried chives
2	Tablespoons dried thyme
2	Tablespoons dried dill

Directions

1. Mix together in a large plastic bag.
2. Store in a cool dry place for use in recipes such as Stuart's focaccia bread or for homemade crackers.

Beef Spice Mix

Makes almost 2 cups

Ingredients

½	cup dried parsley
1/3	cup dried thyme
½	cup dried chives
2	teaspoons ground white pepper
1	Tablespoon garlic powder
1/3	cup dried tarragon
2½	Tablespoons dried basil

Directions

1. Mix together in a large plastic bag.
2. Store in a cool dry place for use in recipes.

Chili Spice Mix

Makes 1 cup

Ingredients

¼	cup ground cayenne pepper or ground chili peppers
1	teaspoon crushed dried red pepper
½	cup paprika
2	Tablespoons onion powder
4	teaspoons cumin seeds
2	teaspoons dried ground oregano
2	teaspoons Kosher salt
2	teaspoons garlic powder

Directions

1. Combine all ingredients.
2. Mix well and store in an airtight container.
3. Use about 2 to 4 Tablespoons for each one pound of meat when making chili, depending on your palate.

PORK SPICE MIX

Makes 2½ cups

Ingredients

- ¼ cup garlic powder
- ¼ cup lemon pepper
- ¼ cup ground black pepper
- ½ cup parsley flakes
- ¼ cup dried chives
- ¼ cup dry mustard
- ¼ cup dried thyme
- ¼ cup dried tarragon
- ¼ cup dried sage

Directions

1. Combine all ingredients in an airtight container.
2. Label container and store in a cool dry environment.
3. Use to season pork roasts.

LAMB RUB

Makes 1½ cups

Ingredients

- ¼ cup dried thyme
- ¼ cup dried sage
- ¼ cup dried marjoram
- ¼ cup dried rosemary
- ¼ cup salt
- ¼ cup ground pepper

Directions

1. Combine all ingredients in an airtight container or large plastic bag.
2. Label container and store in a cool dry environment.
3. Rub lamb with oil and coat with mix before roasting.

CREOLE SPICE MIX

Makes 1 cup

Ingredients

- 3½ Tablespoons paprika
- 2 Tablespoons garlic powder
- 1 Tablespoon onion powder
- 1½ Tablespoons cayenne powder
- 1 Tablespoon dried oregano
- 1 Tablespoon dried thyme
- 1 Tablespoon black pepper
- 2 Tablespoons kosher salt

Directions

1. Combine all ingredients in an airtight container or large plastic bag.
2. Mix until completely blended.
3. Use on meat, rice or in sauces for that spicy Louisiana flair.

Garam Masala

Makes ¼ cup

Ingredients

- 1 Tablespoon ground cumin
- 1½ teaspoons ground coriander
- 1½ teaspoons ground cardamom
- 1 teaspoon fennel
- 1½ teaspoons ground black pepper
- 1 teaspoon ground cinnamon
- ½ teaspoon ground cloves
- ½ teaspoon ground nutmeg
- ½ teaspoon chili pepper flakes

Directions

1. In a coffee grinder or with a mortar and pestle, combine all spices together and grind to a fine powder.
2. Store in an airtight container up to 6 months.

Chef's tip

Our garam masala is one of many variations of this Indian spice. Cooks add or delete ingredients according to their family's taste. It's great sprinkled over vegetables, meat, fish or cooked with rice for an exotic flair.

Blackening Spice Mix

Makes 1¼ cups

Ingredients

- 1 cup paprika
- 1 Tablespoon salt
- 1 Tablespoon ground black pepper
- 1 Tablespoon chili powder
- 1 Tablespoon garlic powder

Directions

1. Combine all ingredients in an airtight container or large plastic zipper bag.
2. Label container and store in a cool dry environment.
3. Use on fish or chicken before cooking.

Roux

A roux is a mixture of fat and flour that has been slowly cooked over low heat until the flour taste is gone. It is used as a thickening agent for soups and sauces. There are three basic roux—white, blond and brown. I use the white roux to make basic white sauces like béchamel or cheese sauce. I use the blond roux, made with butter, for thickening light colored soups. To make brown roux, I use rendered fat in place of butter for sauce or gravy with meat dishes.

Ingredients

1 cup butter

1¾ cups white flour

Or for larger batches, *weigh* out equal parts of fat and flour

Directions

1. Melt 1 cup butter or fat in a saucepan over medium heat.
2. Once the fat is melted, add 1¾ cups white flour, stirring constantly until a thick, rough paste forms.
3. As the roux keeps cooking, it will become smooth and begin to thin.
4. Once the flour loses its raw smell, after about 5 to 6 minutes of cooking, you have a white roux.
5. For blond roux, continue cooking and stirring for another 10 to 20 minutes, or until the roux turns a rich golden color with a very smooth texture and much thinner than it was at the white stage.
6. For a brown roux, continue cooking until it becomes a deep brown paste with a nutty aroma.
7. Some cooks take the roux one step further, to the dark brown stage which occurs after about 45 minutes of cooking. This roux will no longer bubble and will be very thin and dark brown in color. The aroma will be a bit more mellow with the tiniest hint of chocolate.

A roux goes through various levels of color changes during the cooking process, as demonstrated in the accompanying photos.

Sauces And Gravies

Pork Gravy

Makes 6½ cups

Ingredients

1	teaspoon dry mustard
1	teaspoon garlic powder
1	teaspoon white pepper
1	teaspoon salt
6	pork bouillon cubes (use chicken bouillon if pork is not available)
6	cups milk
½	cup blond roux

Directions

1. Heat roux in a two-quart saucepan until hot.
2. Add spices.
3. Add milk, one cup at a time, and stir until smooth and bubbling between each addition of milk.
4. For a thicker gravy, use less milk.

Sausage Gravy

Makes 5 cups

Ingredients

1	pound pork or turkey sausage
4	cups whole milk
½	cup flour
½	Tablespoon pork bouillon (or chicken bouillon if pork is not available)

Directions

1. Fry sausage into crumbles. Do not drain.
2. Add flour.
3. When mixed well, add milk a little at a time and stir between each addition to keep lumps from forming.
4. When it starts to thicken, add bouillon. Stir well.
5. Serve over biscuits.

White Sauce

Makes 2 cups

Ingredients

- 4 Tablespoons flour
- 2 Tablespoons butter
- 3 cups milk
- 1 cube chicken bouillon
- 1 teaspoon pepper
- ½ teaspoon salt or to taste

Directions

1. Melt butter in saucepan.
2. Add flour and stir until smooth to create a white roux (or use pre-made roux).
3. Add salt, chicken bouillon and then milk very slowly, stirring constantly.
4. Cook and stir until smooth and thick, 10 to 12 minutes.

Chef's tip

This is no-rules cooking! Try adding meat from a roasted chicken to the white sauce and serve over biscuits for a quick meal.

The mushroom sauce below makes a nice gravy for country fried steak or chicken.

Mushroom Sauce

Makes 2 cups

Ingredients

- 2 cups white sauce (see recipe above)
- ¼ pound mushrooms, sliced
- 1 Tablespoon butter

Directions

1. Sauté mushrooms in butter until golden brown.
2. Add to white sauce recipe (see directions above) and simmer for 2 to 3 minutes.

CHEESE SAUCE
Makes 2 cups

Ingredients

3	cups milk
2	Tablespoons onion powder
2	ounces cheddar cheese
1	ounce parmesan cheese
½	teaspoon lemon pepper
1	teaspoon white pepper
6	whole peppercorns, crushed
¼	cup blond roux for thickening

Directions

1. In 2-quart saucepan, heat roux.
2. Add milk a little at a time, stirring after each addition until smooth and all milk is used.
3. Bring to a boil, stirring constantly.
4. Lower heat.
5. Add remaining ingredients, stirring constantly until smooth.
6. Serve over vegetables, macaroni, or use as a base for scalloped potatoes.

PONZU SAUCE
Makes 2½ cups

Ingredients

7	ounces Hoisin Sauce
1½	cups pineapple juice
3	Tablespoons rice wine vinegar
3	Tablespoons soy sauce
6	Tablespoons Teriyaki Sauce
1½	Tablespoons cornstarch

Directions

1. Mix 2 Tablespoons of pineapple juice with cornstarch to make a slurry.
2. In a medium sauce pan, mix remaining ingredients and bring to a boil.
3. Add cornstarch slurry, stirring until the sauce boils and thickens.
4. Serve with noodles and grilled fish.

SAFFRON CREAM SAUCE
Makes about 2 cups

Ingredients

1	Tablespoon butter
¼	cup shallots, chopped
5-6	threads saffron
1	bay leaf
1	cup white wine
1	Tablespoon lobster base
2	cups heavy cream
	Salt and pepper to taste
1	Tablespoon cornstarch
½	cup water

Directions

1. Sauté shallots, saffron and bay leaf in butter.
2. Deglaze with white wine.
3. Add lobster base, cream, salt and pepper.
4. Bring to a boil and simmer for 2 to 3 minutes.
5. Meanwhile, make a slurry with cornstarch and water.
6. Add slurry to sauce while still simmering; whisk well.
7. Remove bay leaf before serving over fish or lobster.

Cherry Pepper Sauce

Makes 3 cups

Ingredients

1	Tablespoon olive oil
1-2	shallots, diced
½	cup dried cherries
¼	cup dried cranberries
¼	cup raspberries
½	cup sugar
¼	cup balsamic vinegar
½	cup red wine
2	cups water
2	Tablespoons green peppercorns
1	bay leaf
1	Tablespoon cornstarch
½	cup water

Directions

1. Sauté diced shallots in olive oil until translucent.
2. Add next 9 ingredients and simmer in saucepan for 20 to 30 minutes.
3. If a thicker sauce is desired, mix 1 Tablespoon cornstarch with ½ cup water, and whisk it into the sauce as it boils.
4. Use over fish or duck.

Spring Roll Dipping Sauce

Makes 2 cups

Ingredients

1	cup soy sauce
¾	cup sweet and sour sauce
½	cup rice wine vinegar
1½	teaspoons sesame oil
¾	teaspoon sesame seeds
2	thin slices of scallions for garnish

Directions

1. Combine soy sauce, sweet and sour sauce, rice wine vinegar and sesame oil.
2. Bring to boil and simmer 20 minutes.
3. Add sesame seeds, stirring well.
4. Top with scallions for garnish.

Satay Sauce

Makes about 2½ cups

Ingredients

4	Tablespoons peanut oil
1½	Tablespoons garlic, minced
2	Tablespoons onion, minced
1	teaspoon red pepper flakes
1	teaspoon curry paste, red or green
1	Tablespoon fresh lemon grass, diced very fine
1	12-ounce can coconut milk
¾	cup whole milk or heavy cream
1	Tablespoon fish sauce
¼	cup peanut butter or other nut butter
3	Tablespoons soy sauce
3	Tablespoons lime juice
3	Tablespoons light brown sugar

Directions

1. Sauté garlic, onion, red pepper flakes, curry paste and lemon grass in peanut oil.
2. Stir in remaining ingredients.
3. Bring to a boil, then reduce about 20 percent.

The Prepared Cook

Sambal Dipping Sauce
Makes 3 cups

Ingredients

1¾	cups water
1	cup rice vinegar
1	small carrot, grated
½	cup sambal chili sauce
1	Tablespoon sugar
	Salt and pepper to taste
½	Tablespoon cornstarch
¼	cup water

Directions

1. In a sauce pan bring all ingredients except cornstarch and ¼ cup water to a boil.
2. Make a slurry with cornstarch and ¼ cup water.
3. Whisk slurry into boiling mixture and continue stirring for about 1 to 2 minutes.
4. Makes a good dipping sauce for sushi and spring rolls.

Chef's tip

This sauce may be used as a dipping sauce or for basting grilled chicken or beef. I like to take thinly sliced strips of chicken and thread them on a skewer that has been soaked in water for 30 minutes. Grill the chicken until done and top with sambal dipping sauce.

Malted Mint Sauce

Makes 3 cups

Ingredients

- 12 ounces malt vinegar
- 1 cup sugar
- 1 cup fresh mint, coarsely chopped

Directions

1. Bring all ingredients to a boil in saucepan.
2. Lower heat and simmer for 30 minutes.
3. Strain into a container and store unused portion in the refrigerator.
4. This sauce is a nice change from mint jelly on your lamb chops.

Roasted Red Pepper Sauce

Makes 3½ cups

Ingredients

- 1 clove garlic, chopped
- 2 Tablespoons olive oil
- 4 roasted red peppers, skinned and cleaned
- ½ cup chicken stock
- 1½ cups olive oil

Directions

1. Sauté garlic and roasted red peppers in 2 Tablespoons olive oil.
2. When garlic is slightly browned, deglaze pan with chicken stock.
3. Remove from heat and pour into blender.
4. Blend on high speed, slowly adding remaining oil until mixture is emulsified.
5. Serve as a topping for fish, crab cakes or grits. Makes a great plate garnish.

Chef's tip

To make a spinach sauce, follow directions for roasted red pepper sauce, substituting 1 cup packed fresh spinach for red pepper.

Lobster Sauce

Makes 2½ cups

Ingredients

- ½ Tablespoon butter
- 2 Tablespoons chopped shallots
- Pinch Saffron
- 1 bay leaf
- ½ cup white wine
- 1½ Tablespoon lobster base
- 2 cups heavy cream
- Salt and pepper to taste
- 1 teaspoon cornstarch
- 1 Tablespoon water

Directions

1. Sauté shallots, saffron and bay leaf in butter.
2. Add white wine to deglaze.
3. Add lobster base and heavy cream; simmer for 10 minutes.
4. Make slurry of cornstarch and water, then add to above mixture.
5. Simmer until thickened; remove bay leaf before serving.
6. Use while still warm or refrigerate and reheat later.

This sauce goes well with fish, crab cakes or lobster.

Pesto

Makes 1 cup

Ingredients

- 2 cups fresh basil leaves, packed
- ½ cup freshly grated hard cheese (Parmesan, Romano, etc.)
- ½ cup extra virgin olive oil
- ½ cup pine nuts (if unavailable use walnuts)
- 3 garlic cloves
- Sea salt and freshly ground black pepper to taste

Directions

1. Combine basil and pine nuts in food processor and pulse a few times.
2. Add garlic, pulsing a few more times.
3. Drizzle in olive oil in a constant stream while the food processor is on, stopping occasionally to scrape sides to better incorporate ingredients.
4. Add grated cheese and pulse again until blended.
5. Add sea salt and freshly ground black pepper to taste.

Chef's tip

This is a versatile sauce traditionally used to toss with pasta. I often substitute or add mint, cilantro, or sun-dried tomatoes to the pesto. Try serving over baked potatoes or in place of butter on bread or on crostini as an hors d'oeuvre.

BARBECUE SAUCE

Makes about 4 cups

Ingredients

- 2 cups ketchup
- 1/3 cup yellow mustard
- ¾ teaspoon crushed garlic or garlic powder
- ¼ teaspoon beef bouillon
- 2 Tablespoons brown sugar
- 1½ Tablespoons white sugar
- 1 Tablespoon pepper
- 1½ Tablespoons Worcestershire sauce
- 1½ Tablespoons cayenne pepper
- ½ teaspoon hot sauce
- ½ teaspoon soy sauce
- 1/3 cup water
- 1 small onion, chopped
- 1 cup molasses

Directions

1. In a medium sauce pan, combine all ingredients and bring to a boil for a few minutes.
2. Simmer for 10 minutes.
3. Allow to cool.
4. Puree sauce in a blender until smooth.
5. Use immediately or refrigerate for later use.

Chef's tip

This barbecue sauce is great on chicken, pork or beef. I like to use this sauce to simmer my pulled pork or beef for sandwiches.

Serve the amaretto sauce below over almond crusted grouper, sea bass or other whitefish.

AMARETTO SAUCE FOR FISH

Makes 1 cup

Ingredients

- 3 Tablespoons diced shallots
- 1 Tablespoon butter
- 3 Tablespoons brown sugar
- 3 Tablespoons amaretto
- 1 cup chicken stock
- 2 Tablespoons cornstarch
- 6 Tablespoons sliced almonds

Directions

1. Mix cornstarch with ¼ cup cold chicken stock and set aside.
2. In a sauce pan, sauté shallots in butter.
3. Add remaining ingredients and bring to a boil.
4. Add cornstarch slurry and stir to thicken.

The Prepared Cook

Raspberry Sauce
Makes about 2 cups

Ingredients

1	12-ounce package frozen raspberries
¾	cup dry white wine
½	Tablespoon cornstarch

Directions

1. Combine raspberries, cornstarch, and wine in a sauce pan over medium heat.
2. Cook until mixture starts to simmer and remove from heat.
3. With a masher, force mixture through a sieve, taking care not to crush seeds as this will make a tart sauce.
4. Strain mixture once again and refrigerate.
5. Use as a plate sauce for desserts or drizzle over duck and game dishes.
6. If you prefer a sweeter sauce add corn syrup to taste.

Simple Syrup
Makes 3 cups

Ingredients

3	cups water
1	cup sugar
1	teaspoon vanilla or maple flavoring (optional)

Directions

1. In saucepan combine water and sugar.
2. Cook over low heat until sugar turns clear.
3. Bring to a boil and boil for one minute.
4. For thicker syrup add 1 to 2 cups extra sugar.
5. For a great pancake syrup, add a teaspoon of vanilla or maple flavoring.

"Did someone say pancakes for breakfast?"

RED ONION MARMALADE
Makes about 4 cups

Ingredients

7	medium red onions sliced thin
2	ounces olive oil
¾	cup red wine vinegar
¼	cup balsamic vinegar
3	cups sugar
¼	cup water
	Pinch of salt

Directions

1. Preheat a non-stick pan on high, add oil and then the onions.
2. Sauté for 2 minutes.
3. Add sugar, red wine vinegar, balsamic vinegar and water.
4. Bring to a boil, then turn heat down and let reduce for about 20 minutes.
5. Cool immediately.

Chef's tip

Both condiments on this page may be stored in refrigerator for use as a spread or topping on hamburgers, sandwiches, chicken, fish or even steaks and chops.

REMOULADE SAUCE
Makes 1 quart

Ingredients

3	cups mayonnaise
3-4	Tablespoons capers, washed and drained
3-4	Tablespoons sour pickles, finely chopped
3-4	chives, finely chopped
3-4	Tablespoons fresh tarragon, finely chopped
1-2	Tablespoons Dijon mustard
3-4	anchovies, mashed into paste
1	Tablespoon Worcestershire
1	Tablespoon Tabasco sauce
1	Tablespoon lemon juice
	Salt to taste

Directions

1. Mix all ingredients in a stainless steel bowl until well blended.
2. Keep refrigerated.

Walnut Chutney

Makes 3½ cups

Ingredients

- ½ cup sugar
- 2½ cups water
- 4 sprigs fresh thyme, de-stemmed and chopped
- 1½ Granny Smith apples, peeled, cored, and diced
- 1 cup walnuts
- 2 heaping Tablespoons cornstarch mixed with ½ cup water to make a slurry

Directions

1. Toast walnuts in pan until just brown.
2. Add remaining ingredients except slurry.
3. Bring to a boil for 10 to 15 minutes until apples are tender.
4. Add cornstarch slurry.
5. Whisk until thickened.
6. Store in airtight container in refrigerator until use. Serve as a side dish with cheese or as a topping for fish, chicken or pork.

Beurre Blanc Sauce

Makes 2 cups

Ingredients

- 1 shallot, diced
- 2 ounces white wine
- 2 Tablespoons lemon or orange juice
- 2 s heavy cream
- 1 stick butter, softened

Directions

1. In saucepan, sauté diced shallot in 1 Tablespoon of the butter until translucent.
2. Add white wine and lemon juice.
3. Cook over high heat to reduce by 50 percent.
4. Add cream.
5. Reduce another 10 to 20 percent.
6. Remove from heat and whisk in remaining softened butter.
7. Serve immediately over chicken, fish or vegetables.

Hollandaise Sauce in a Jiffy

Makes 3/4 cup

Ingredients

- 3 egg yolks
- 1 Tablespoon lemon juice
- ½ teaspoon salt
- Dash cayenne pepper
- ½ cup bubbling hot butter

Directions

1. In blender, combine egg yolks, lemon juice, salt and cayenne.
2. Blend until smooth.
3. While blender is still running, gradually add hot butter in a steady stream until thick and creamy.
4. Serve immediately.

Yellow Dog Café ™ Cookbook

Rocket Mayo

Makes ¾ cup

Ingredients

2	Tablespoons wasabi
½	cup mayonnaise
1	anchovy (optional), mashed
5	capers
1	pinch salt
1	Tablespoon lemon or lime juice
4	Tablespoons sour cream
4	Tablespoons heavy cream
¼	teaspoon Worcestershire sauce
2	drops hot sauce or to taste

Directions

1. Whisk all ingredients together.
2. Refrigerate until ready for use as a spread on sandwiches or for a spicy twist in tuna or chicken salad.

Lime and Ginger Glaze

Makes 1¼ cups

Ingredients

¼	pound fresh ginger, scrubbed and grated
2	shallots, diced
1	Tablespoon olive oil
1	cup sugar
2	cup water
	Lime juice to taste
	Salt and pepper to taste

Directions

1. In saucepan, sauté ginger and shallots in olive oil.
2. Add sugar and caramelize.
3. Add water and reduce by 50 percent.
4. Add salt, pepper and lime juice to taste.

Salsa

Makes 2 cups

Ingredients

- 2 tomatoes, diced
- ½ red onion, diced
- ¼ cup chopped cilantro
- ½ green pepper, diced
- 1 Tablespoon jalapeño pepper, chopped
- Juice of one lemon
- Salt and pepper to taste

Directions

1. Combine all ingredients and mix well.
2. Serve chilled or un-chilled with your favorite corn chips or use as a topping for grilled fish.

Black Bean & Mango Salsa

Makes 5 cups

Ingredients

- 1 diced red onion
- 1 cup diced tomatoes
- 1 cup diced mango
- 1 1-pound can drained and rinsed black beans
- ¼ cup chopped cilantro
- Juice of one lime
- 1 Tablespoon corn syrup (optional)
- Salt and pepper to taste

Directions

1. Combine all ingredients, sweeten with corn syrup if necessary.
2. Serve as a dip for corn chips, as a side dish or as a topping for fish.

Photo by John Sluter

Breads and Batters

Potato Rolls
Makes 3 dozen rolls

Ingredients

1	cup milk, lukewarm
1	cup warm mashed potatoes
½	cup shortening
¼	cup sugar
2	teaspoons salt
2¼	teaspoons dry yeast
½	cup water, lukewarm
2	eggs, beaten
6½	cups flour
1	Tablespoon olive oil or melted butter

Directions

1. Preheat oven to 425° F.
2. Combine water, milk, sugar and yeast in mixing bowl.
3. Let stand until foamy.
4. Add mashed potatoes, shortening, eggs and flour; using a dough hook, mix on low speed until elastic.
5. Cover and let stand until double in size.
6. Knead lightly on floured surface until smooth.
7. Divide into 36 individual pieces, about one inch in diameter.
8. Shape each piece into a round ball.
9. Place on greased cookie sheets about two inches apart.
10. Spray or brush tops with olive oil or melted butter.
11. Let rise 1 to 1¼ hours or until double in size.
12. Bake at 425° F for 10 to 12 minutes.
13. Brush with butter and serve.

Bistro Cinnamon Rolls

Makes 12 large rolls

Chef's tip

If dough becomes hard to stretch or roll, allow it to rest for five to ten minutes before continuing to shape.

Ingredients

Dough

2	cups warm water
1	cup milk
1	Tablespoon yeast
1	egg
7	cups flour
½	cup sugar
½	teaspoon salt
5/8	cup shortening
1	egg plus ¼ cup milk, blended for brushing top of buns

Filling

1	stick softened butter
1¼	cup sugar
2	Tablespoons cinnamon

Directions

1. Dissolve yeast in warm water with sugar and milk until it foams.
2. In separate bowl whip egg.
3. Once yeast has bubbled, combine with egg.
4. In a large mixing bowl combine flour and salt.
5. Add yeast/water/milk/egg mixture and shortening to flour.
6. Mix well and knead by hand or a dough hook until dough is elastic.
7. Place dough in a large greased bowl; let rise in a warm place until double, about 1 hour, then knock down.
8. Let rest for 10 minutes before shaping dough with rolling pin into a 15 X 24 -inch rectangle.
9. Spread softened butter over dough.
10. Mix cinnamon and sugar and sprinkle over the butter.
11. Roll, starting from the wide side, into a log.
12. Cut log into 2-inch circles and arrange in large cake pan or jelly roll pan.
13. Brush with egg wash.
14. Let proof in warm place again until doubled in size.
15. Bake at 325°F for 10 to 15 minutes.
16. Spread with icing of choice if desired (see page 166).
17. Serve warm or cold.

Sticky Buns

Makes 9 buns

Ingredients

- 1 Tablespoon dry yeast
- ½ cup water, 105° to 115°F
- ½ cup warm milk
- 1/3 cup sugar
- ½ cup softened butter plus
- 2 Tablespoons butter for greasing pan
- ½ teaspoon salt
- 1 egg, beaten
- 3½ cups flour, sifted
- 1 egg plus ¼ cup milk, blended for brushing top of buns

Sticky Bun Filling

- ½ cup granulated sugar
- ¾ cup light brown sugar
- 1 Tablespoon cinnamon
- 1 stick butter

Heat all ingredients on low in sauce pan until mixture is smooth. Do not boil. Set aside and let cool.

Directions

1. Dissolve yeast in warm water and milk and allow to bubble.
2. Measure flour and salt into a large mixing bowl.
3. Make a well in center and add sugar, ¼ cup melted butter, egg, and yeast mixture.
4. Mix well and knead by hand (or mixer with dough hook) and shape into a ball.
5. Cover dough with a kitchen towel and allow to rise until double.
6. Punch down.
7. Roll out into a 9 X 18 - inch rectangle.
8. Brush sheet of dough with remaining butter.
9. Pour sticky bun filling over rectangle and smooth evenly across dough
10. Roll up into an 18 inch long log. Cut log into 2-inch rounds.
11. Grease a 9 X 12 cake pan with 2 Tablespoons butter and place buns in pan.
12. Top with any remaining sticky bun filling that may have oozed out when you rolled dough into log.
13. Brush with egg wash.
14. Allow buns to proof until doubled.
15. Bake in preheated 325° F oven for 15 to 18 minutes or until golden brown.
16. Invert onto platter and serve warm.

Basic Dough for Meat Pies

Makes 24 meat pies

Ingredients

6	cups flour
1¼	teaspoon salt
½	cup oil
¼	cup butter
1	Tablespoon yeast
2½	cups warm water
½	teaspoon sugar

Directions

1. Mix yeast with ½ cup warm water and sugar; set aside.
2. Place flour and salt in mixing bowl.
3. In a measuring cup, melt butter and add remaining water and oil.
4. In mixing bowl with flour and salt, add yeast mixture, then butter/water/oil mixture and knead until smooth.
5. Cover and keep in warm place for 2 to 3 hours.
6. Cut dough into 24 balls and place on floured cookie sheet.
7. Let stand one hour before using.
8. With fingertips, flatten balls until thin.
9. Place about 1 Tablespoon pre-made filling (see pages 33 and 134 for recipes) on one half, wet edges of dough, fold over and seal with tines of fork.
10. Bake in a preheated 425° F oven for 8 to 10 minutes or until done.

Chef's tip

Any leftover dough, may be frozen for later use.

CHEESE BREAD
Makes 6 loaves

Chef's tip

Instead of onion, use chopped chives or scallions, chopped parsley and some spices like paprika, coriander or cumin. You may also use a variety of cheeses, grated and blended together.

Ingredients

1	pound Feta cheese
2	onions, finely diced or grated
4	teaspoons soft butter
½	cup flour
	Basic dough for meat pies (see previous page)

Directions

1. Mash cheese, onions, butter and flour together.
2. Separate basic dough into six round balls and flatten onto lightly greased cookie sheet.
3. Spread cheese mixture on flattened dough.
4. Let proof for one hour.
5. Bake at 425° F for about 7 minutes or until done.

BISCUITS
Makes 24

Ingredients

1	cup butter, margarine or Crisco shortening
4	cups flour
2	Tablespoons sugar
2½	Tablespoons baking powder
½	teaspoon salt
1	scant cup buttermilk
	Egg wash

Directions

1. Combine dry ingredients.
2. Add softened butter and mix until crumbly.
3. Add milk and mix until just combined.
4. Turn dough onto lightly floured surface, pressing with fingertips until about 1 inch thick.
5. Cut into circles, place on lightly greased cookie sheet, egg wash and bake at 350° F for 9 minutes.

Serve with orange blossom honey from Florida.

Yellow Dog Café ™ Cookbook

Soft Bread Rolls
Makes 12 rolls

Ingredients

½	cup water at 105°F to 115°F
½	cup milk at 105°F to 115°F
1	Tablespoon yeast at room temperature
3½	cups plus ½ cup flour reserved for adjustments
¼	cup sugar
½	cup shortening
½	teaspoon salt
1	egg at room temperature
1	egg beaten mixed with ¼ cup water for egg wash
¼	cup butter, melted for brushing top of rolls after baking

Directions

1. Dissolve yeast in warm milk, water and sugar, then allow to bubble.
2. Add shortening.
3. Mix dry ingredients in separate bowl.
4. Whip egg into yeast mixture.
5. Add dry ingredients and mix well with a dough hook until you have a firm ball.
6. Allow to proof for 1 to 1½ hours. Knock down and make 12 round balls. Place on a greased cookie sheet about 1 inch apart.
7. Set aside to rise in a warm environment.
8. When doubled, brush tops with egg wash before baking in a preheated 325°F oven for 10 to 15 minutes or until done.
9. Brush with melted butter and serve warm.

Chef's tip

This recipe is extremely versatile. Instead of making rolls, shape this dough into a loaf, place in greased bread pan or shape into a long bun on a cookie sheet; let rise until double. Egg wash top and bake at 325° F for 15 to 18 minutes.

Beignet (fried dough): Use the above recipe. After the first rising, flatten dough into ½ inch thickness. Cut into 2-inch squares, then let proof until doubled. Deep fry until golden brown, turning once. Drain quickly on paper towel and immediately coat with powdered sugar and serve.

Focaccia Bread
(House Flatbread)
Makes 2 cookie sheets; serves 24

Ingredients

2	cups water at 105° to 115°F
1	Tablespoon sugar
1	Tablespoon dry yeast
¼	cup oil
6	cups flour
2	teaspoons salt
3	Tablespoons house spice mix (see page 26)

Directions

1. Dissolve yeast and sugar in warm water and allow to bubble.
2. Mix flour, salt and spices together in large bowl.
3. Add oil and yeast mixture.
4. Knead until smooth.
5. Divide into two balls.
6. Let proof until doubled.
7. Press and spread each ball by hand into an 11 X 18-inch cookie sheet. If it becomes too hard to spread, allow dough to rest for 10 minutes before resuming the shaping process. It's okay to have fingerprints on the dough.
8. Brush dough with olive oil.
9. Sprinkle with additional spice mix and Kosher salt.
10. Let proof again.
11. Bake in a preheated oven at 325° F for 15 to 18 minutes until golden brown.
12. After cooling, cut in squares for serving.

Chef's tip

This is a versatile bread. It may be topped with Parmesan cheese before baking or add olives to the dough as you make it or place olives on top before baking. For thin crust sandwiches, slice the squares and use like a hamburger bun.

Nancy's Zucchini Bread

Makes two loaves; serves 12 - 16

Ingredients

1	cup oil
3	eggs
2	cups grated zucchini, seeded
2	cups sugar
2	teaspoons vanilla
1	teaspoon baking soda
¼	teaspoon baking powder
3	cups flour
1	teaspoon salt
1	teaspoon cinnamon

Directions

1. Preheat oven to 350° F.
2. Mix all ingredients well.
3. Pour into two well-greased bread pans.
4. Bake in center of oven at 350° F for 55 to 60 minutes.

Italian Bread

Makes one 1-pound loaf; serves 6

Ingredients

3	cups bread flour
1	Tablespoon vegetable oil
½	teaspoon yeast
½	teaspoon salt
1¼	cups warm water

Directions

1. Activate yeast in warm water.
2. Add salt and oil.
3. Add flour and mix well with dough hook.
4. Set aside and allow to proof two times, punching down after each proofing.
5. Grease a loaf pan with oil.
6. Shape dough into loaf and place in pan.
7. Let proof again.
8. Brush top with oil and bake at 325° F for 15 to 20 minutes.

Nancy's Pizza Dough

Makes 2 16-inch pizza rounds; serves 8

Ingredients

4	cups flour plus ½ cup for adjustments
1	Tablespoon plus 1 teaspoon yeast
1	Tablespoon sugar
1	teaspoon salt
2	cups water
1½	Tablespoons oil for dough
1	Tablespoon oil for greasing each pan

Chef's tip

Grate mozzarella straight from the block onto the pizza. Try my personal favorite by using Havarti cheese instead of traditional mozzarella cheese. Top with fresh grated parmesan.

Directions

1. Activate yeast in warm water and sugar until the mixture bubbles.
2. Add salt, oil and then the flour.
3. Mix well using dough hook. If dough is too sticky, add 1 Tablespoon flour at a time until the dough comes away from the side of the bowl.
4. Divide into two balls. Set aside on sheet pan and allow to proof.
5. Once doubled, start shaping the pizza rounds, stopping along the way to give the dough a 1 minute rest before pushing the dough into its final 16-inch size.
6. Using fork tines, poke holes all over dough to eliminate bubbles.
7. Allow to rise a few minutes before topping with 6 ounces of sauce and your favorite pizza toppings before covering with 6 to 8 ounces of grated cheese.

Chef's tip

Separate out the amount of dough you intend to use after the first proofing. Roll the remainder into balls and freeze dough for future use. You can also use some of the remaining dough to make fried dough for dessert or garlic knots.

Stuart's Tempura Batter

Makes 4½ cups batter

Ingredients

½	pound sifted flour (about 1¾ cups to 2 cups)
1	egg
4	cups cold soda water
2	Tablespoons salt
1	Tablespoon white pepper
1	teaspoon cayenne pepper
1	Tablespoon garlic powder

Directions

1. Blend all ingredients together until smooth.
2. Use as a batter for frying shrimp, chicken or tempura style vegetables such as asparagus, sliced zucchini, yellow squash, shredded carrots or mushrooms.

Chef's tip

Dredging meat or vegetables in plain flour or cornstarch before coating with batter will help the batter stick better. I like to set aside some batter to make vegetable patties (see recipe for carrot patties on page 121).

Yellow Dog Dry Fry Mix

Makes 3½ cups dry mix

Ingredients

- 2 cups flour
- ½ cup extra fine cornmeal
- ½ cup powdered milk
- 3 Tablespoons lemon pepper
- 1 Tablespoon baking powder
- 1 Tablespoon salt
- 1 teaspoon Old Bay seasoning
- 1 Tablespoon paprika

Directions

1. Mix all ingredients together and store in an airtight container.
2. For a light breading, dredge meat, fish or vegetables in dry fry mix before frying.

To make use of the full batch of fry mix, use 2 to 2 ½ cups water.

Yellow Dog Fry Batter

Makes ¾ cup batter

Ingredients

- 1 cup Yellow Dog Dry Fry mix (see recipe above)
- ½ cup water

Directions

1. Measure fry mix into a large bowl.
2. Add water and blend well.
3. Use to coat onions, meat or potato balls for frying.

Corn Fritters

Makes about 30

Ingredients

- 1 cup flour
- 2 Tablespoons baking powder
- 1½ cups sugar
- 2 cups frozen corn
- 1 cup red peppers, chopped
- 1½ cup white onions, chopped
- 1 egg
- ¼ cup milk

Dipping sauce

- 1 Tablespoon sambal chili sauce
- ½ cup corn syrup
- 1 teaspoon lime juice

Combine all three ingredients, stir and serve with corn fritters.

Directions

1. Mix all dry ingredients together.
2. Add chopped vegetables and mix.
3. Add egg and mix.
4. Add milk little by little; batter should be fairly thick.
5. To cook, drop in 350° F oil by tablespoon, using back of another spoon to slide off, cooking in small batches until golden brown.
6. Drain on paper towels and serve.

Crepe Batter

Makes 12

Ingredients

1½	cups flour
1	Tablespoon sugar
½	teaspoon baking powder
½	teaspoon salt
2	cups milk
2	Tablespoons melted butter
½	teaspoon vanilla
2	eggs
1	8-ounce jar fruit preserves or other filling

See recipe for Apple Cinnamon Crepes on page 160.

Directions

1. Mix flour, sugar, salt and baking powder; add remaining ingredients and mix well in blender or mixer.
2. Pour 1/8 cup of batter into medium hot non-stick skillet.
3. Cook until firm, then flip and cook until done (approximately 30 seconds).
4. Stack on top of one another and keep warm until needed. Unused crepes may be frozen. Place a layer of parchment paper between crepes before freezing.
5. Add 2 to 3 tablespoons of fruit preserves or other desired filling onto each crepe and spread evenly. Fold crepe in half and then half again. Place desired number of crepes on plate and top with your favorite sauce or syrup.

The Prepared Cook

Pancake/Waffle Batter

Makes 6 to 8 pancakes

Ingredients

2	cups flour
1	teaspoon salt
¼	cup sugar
1	teaspoon baking soda
1	teaspoon baking powder
2	cups buttermilk (or substitute 1 Tablespoon vinegar mixed with milk)
2	eggs, lightly beaten
1	teaspoon vanilla
½	stick melted butter
	Vegetable oil as needed

Directions

1. Combine all ingredients together in mixer bowl.
2. Whip on medium speed until well blended.
3. Add oil if too thick.

For pancakes

1. Pour batter onto medium hot griddle to desired size: 3 to 6 - inch cakes, using a bit of oil if you are not using a non-stick pan.
2. Cook until bubbles form.
3. Flip and cook until batter is done.

For waffles

1. Pour desired amount of batter onto waffle iron, making sure all squares are filled but not overflowing.
2. Close top of griddle and cook until steam stops coming out of waffle griddle.

Chef's tip

A favorite way to serve pancakes in Australia is with strawberries, cream and powdered sugar.

Try American style by adding handfuls of chocolate chips, raisins, fresh blueberries or your favorite dried fruits such as banana or apple chips into the batter.

57

EGGS

How to Make Poached Eggs

1. Bring to boil one quart of water and 1 Tablespoons vinegar and a pinch of salt. Reduce heat until water barely simmers.
2. Break each egg separately into a ramekin or small dish.
3. Lower dish to surface of water and slide eggs gently out.
4. Cook about three minutes for a medium egg, making sure the eggs don't touch each other.
5. You may easily cook four eggs in the quart size saucepan.
6. Using a slotted spoon remove eggs from water, allowing excess water to drip back into the saucepan.
7. Serve immediately.

Chef's tip

If you are cooking for a crowd, don't cram the pan with eggs. Poach in small batches of four to six eggs, slightly undercooking them, about two minutes. Slide them into a large bowl of cold water. When ready to be served, immerse eggs in barely simmering water for 1 to 2 minutes.

Eggs Benedict

Makes one serving

Ingredients

2	eggs, poached
2	slices Canadian bacon, warmed
1	English muffin, split and toasted
½	cup Hollandaise sauce (see recipe on page 40)

Directions

1. Poach two eggs.
2. Toast the English muffins.
3. Top each muffin with a slice of warmed Canadian bacon.
4. Carefully lift each egg out of hot water with slotted spoon, allowing water to drain, and lay it on top of the bacon.
5. Top each egg with a dollop of Hollandaise.
6. Serve immediately.

Eggs

Eggs Jason
Makes 1 serving

Ingredients

2	poached eggs
1	English muffin, split and toasted
¼	pound Andouille sausage, sliced and sautéed
2	poached peeled shrimp, each split lengthwise
2	slices fresh tomatoes
2	dollops Creole Hollandaise sauce

Creole Hollandaise

Stir into Hollandaise sauce (page 40) 2 pinches paprika and 1 pinch each garlic powder, onion powder, cayenne powder, dried oregano, dried thyme, black pepper and kosher salt.

Directions

1. Toast muffin.
2. Place a hot poached egg on each muffin.
3. Sauté sausage and shrimp, drain any residual oil and arrange on top of eggs.
4. Top each with a tomato slice.
5. Place a dollop of Creole Hollandaise sauce to complete
6. Garnish with a pinch of Creole spice mix.
7. Serve immediately.

Yellow Dog Eggs Sardou
Makes 1 serving

Ingredients

2	eggs
1	English muffin, split and toasted
1	cup packed fresh spinach
¼	teaspoon minced garlic
1	Tablespoon olive oil
½	roasted red pepper, sliced
1	medium portobello mushroom, sliced
2	artichoke hearts, diced
½-¾	cup Hollandaise sauce (see recipe on page 40)

Directions

1. Poach eggs.
2. Sauté spinach in oil and garlic.
3. Arrange spinach on serving plate.
4. Place muffins on top of spinach.
5. Sauté mushroom with red pepper.
6. Microwave artichokes until hot. Stir into warm Hollandaise sauce.
7. Top muffins with sautéed mushrooms and red pepper.
8. Add poached eggs and top with artichoke Hollandaise.

Eggs

CRAB & EGG VOL-AU-VENT

Makes four servings

Ingredients

1   sheet puff pastry
4   crab cakes (see recipe on page 123)
4   poached eggs
½   roasted red pepper, diced
4   dollops Hollandaise sauce (See page 40 for basic recipe)
    Egg wash

Directions

1. Preheat oven to 400° F.
2. Brush pastry with egg wash (a mixture of one egg and water or milk, well beaten).
3. Cut eight 4-inch circles from sheet. (See photo on opposite page.)
4. Grease a cookie sheet and set four circles on the sheet. With the second four circles, cut center out with a 3-inch cutter. Stack the resulting 4-inch outer ring directly on top of the first four circles. Place the 3-inch center cut-outs on cookie sheet also, as you will use this for the lid.
5. Bake at 400° F for 10 to 12 minutes or until pastry is golden brown.
6. While pastry is baking, poach eggs and sauté crab cakes.
7. Heat roasted red peppers in microwave and fold into warm Hollandaise sauce.
8. Place pastry shells on plate; set crab cake inside, top with egg and Hollandaise sauce and add lid if desired.
9. Serve immediately.

Basic Quiche

Makes one 9-inch pie; serves 6

Ingredients

1	cup heavy cream
5	eggs
½	teaspoon salt
1/8	teaspoon nutmeg
	Pinch cayenne pepper
1/8	teaspoon black pepper
1	cup parmesan cheese, shredded
2	cups shredded cheese, your choice
2-3	cups total of your favorite vegetables, blanched and drained, then chopped; diced cooked meat such as crisply fried bacon, ham, sausage, chicken, etc. Reserve ¼ cup for topping
1	9-inch pie shell, unbaked (see recipes on page 168)

Directions

1. Make one 9-inch pie shell, bottom only; using fork tines, prick holes across bottom of pie shell.
2. Sprinkle with ½ cup parmesan cheese.
3. Preheat oven to 425° F.
4. In a mixing bowl, whip together cream, eggs, salt, and spices; set aside.
5. In pie shell, spread 1 cup vegetable/meat mixture topped with ¾ cup of shredded cheese.
6. Repeat process with remaining vegetable/meat mixture until layers reach just below the top of the pie shell.
7. Pour cream and egg mixture over top of layers, making sure to cover all ingredients.
8. Sprinkle ½ cup parmesan cheese on top and bake at 425° F for 15 minutes, then reduce oven temperature to 300° F and bake 40 more minutes or until knife comes out clean.
9. Garnish with reserved vegetable/meat mixture and serve.

Chef's tip

Any leftover quiche filling may be used as an egg wash on bread, as dip for French toast, or simply add an extra egg and make scrambled eggs.

Eggs

Omelette Florentine
Makes 1 serving

Ingredients

3	eggs
1	Tablespoon milk
1	cup fresh spinach, coarsely chopped
¼	cup feta cheese
1	Tablespoon oil
	Salt and pepper to taste

Directions

1. Whip eggs and milk by fork or in blender until fluffy.
2. Fold in spinach.
3. Heat oil in 9-inch oven-proof skillet on medium high until hot but not smoking.
4. Pour in egg mixture into skillet.
5. Cook omelette halfway through, then flip in pan.
6. Top with feta cheese.
7. If uncomfortable flipping, remove skillet from heat and place under a broiler and finish cooking, about 2 minutes.
8. Using hot pad, remove pan from oven.
9. Fold omelette in half and slide onto plate.
10. Sprinkle with more feta cheese and serve.

Chef's tip

Try adding cooked and chopped bacon, different cheeses or season your pan with sautéed garlic before adding your egg mixture.

64

Lobster Omelette

Makes 1 serving

Ingredients

3	eggs
1	Tablespoon milk
¼	cup steamed and diced Maine lobster
¼	cup thinly sliced fresh spinach leaves
1	Tablespoon diced artichoke heart
1	Tablespoon red pepper, diced
5	thin slices grilled portobello mushroom
¼	cup shredded Havarti cheese plus extra for garnish
1	Tablespoon oil
	Salt and pepper to taste

Directions

1. Whip eggs by fork or in blender until fluffy.
2. Fold in spinach, lobster, artichoke heart, red pepper and sliced mushroom.
3. Heat oil in 9-inch oven-proof Sauté pan on medium high until hot but not smoking.
4. Pour egg and lobster mixture into skillet.
5. Cook omelette halfway through, then flip in pan.
6. Top with Havarti cheese.
7. If uncomfortable flipping, remove skillet from heat and place under a broiler and finish cooking, about 2 minutes.
8. Using hot pad, remove pan from oven.
9. Fold omelette in half and slide onto plate.
10. Sprinkle with more Havarti cheese.

VEGETABLE FRITTATA MUFFINS
Makes 6 muffins

Ingredients

6	eggs
½	cup milk
¼	teaspoon salt
1/8	teaspoon pepper
1	cup shredded Cheddar cheese (4 ounces)
¾	cup chopped zucchini
¼	cup chopped red bell pepper
2	Tablespoons chopped red onion

Directions

1. Preheat oven to 325° F.
2. Beat eggs, milk, salt and pepper in medium bowl until blended.
3. Add cheese, zucchini, bell pepper and onion; mix well.
4. Spoon into 6 greased muffin cups.
5. Bake until just set, 20 to 22 minutes.
6. Cool on rack 5 minutes.
7. Remove from cups.
8. Serve warm.

Shrimp Frittata Muffins

Makes 6 muffins

Ingredients

6	eggs
½	cup milk
¼	teaspoon salt
1/8	teaspoon pepper
1	cup cooked and chopped shrimp
½	teaspoon Old Bay seasoning
1	cup shredded Cheddar cheese
¼	cup chopped red bell pepper

Directions

1. Heat oven to 325°F.
2. Beat eggs, milk, salt and pepper in medium bowl until blended.
3. Add remaining ingredients and mix well.
4. Spoon into 6 greased muffin cups.
5. Bake in oven until just set, 20 to 22 minutes.
6. Cool on rack 5 minutes.
7. Remove from cups.
8. Serve warm.

Chef's tip

The frittata recipes on these two pages are examples of the flexibility of this recipe. Be creative by replacing shrimp with crisp crumbled bacon, diced ham, shredded cooked lobster, chives, different cheeses or hot peppers. Try adding Mediterranean spices for a different flavor. Another way to add flavor is to butter the inside of the muffin pan and coat with grated parmesan cheese.

Eggs

Spinach Frittata Muffins

Makes 6 muffins

Ingredients

6	eggs
½	cup milk
¼	teaspoon salt
1/8	teaspoon pepper
½	cup shredded mozzarella cheese
1	cup fresh spinach, chopped, blanched and squeezed dry

Directions

1. Preheat oven to 325° F.
2. Beat eggs, milk, salt and pepper in medium bowl until blended.
3. Add cheese and chopped blanched spinach; mix well.
4. Spoon batter into 6 greased muffin cups.
5. Bake in oven until just set, 20 to 22 minutes.
6. Cool on rack 5 minutes.
7. Remove from cups.
8. Serve warm.

Florida Shrimp and Grits
See recipe on page 72

Grits

The origin of grits is rooted in Native American food preparation. Nowadays, grits is a popular southern dish made of corn and traditionally ground by a stone mill.

At Yellow Dog Cafe, we use Falls Mill stone ground grits to make our special Florida shrimp and grits with crawfish pictured on page 69. Falls Mill, in Belvidere, Tennessee, is an operating water powered grain mill with a museum and is on the National Register of Historic Places.

Before getting into the recipes, place stone-ground grits in a bowl, cover with water and stir. The light bran will rise to the top. Carefully pour off the water and light bran, reserving the grits in the bowl. Rinse again if desired before cooking.

Falls Mill Basic Grits
Makes 4 half-cup servings

Ingredients

2	cups water
½	teaspoon salt
1	Tablespoon butter
1	cup grits, prepared as instructed above

Directions

1. In a saucepan, bring 2 cups of water, ½ teaspoon salt and 1 Tablespoon butter to a boil.
2. Stir in grits.
3. Boil for 1 minute then reduce heat to low and simmer covered, about 20 minutes.
4. Stir occasionally until grits are thick and creamy.
5. If too thick, add a little more water or some milk or cream.
6. Serve hot.

Easy Cheese Grits

Makes 12 half-cup servings

Ingredients

4	cups water
1	cup stone-ground grits
2	teaspoons chicken bouillon
2	Tablespoons finely chopped onion (optional)
2	Tablespoons butter
¼	cup half-and-half
2-4	ounces of shredded cheese (American, Cheddar, or Havarti)

Directions

1. Place grits in bowl and cover with 2 cups water.
2. Stir grits so that light bran will rise to the top; carefully pour off the water and bran, reserving the grits in the bowl.
3. Rinse again if desired.
4. Bring 2 cups water, onion, chicken bouillon, and butter to a boil in a saucepan.
5. Add grits to the boiling mixture.
6. Reduce heat to low and cook covered 20 minutes, stirring occasionally until grits are soft and creamy.
7. Add half-and-half and cheese and stir until cheese melts. Serve hot.

Jalapeño Grits

Cook basic grits according to directions on page 70. Add 1½ cups of shredded cheese, 3 tablespoons butter, 2 beaten eggs, chopped jalapeño pepper to taste (start with 2 Tablespoons), salt and pepper to taste. Pour into a greased baking dish, bake at 350° F for about 30 minutes. Top will be lightly browned.

Aloha Grits

Like sweet grits? Try this recipe. Prepare basic grits according to directions on page 70, stir in ¼ cup milk or cream, 4 tablespoons brown sugar, ¼ cup pineapple juice, stir together and pour into a greased baking dish. Sprinkle top with shredded coconut, crushed macadamia nuts and a pinch of ginger. Bake at 350° F for about 30 minutes.

Florida Shrimp and Grits
Serves 12

Ingredients

8	ounces andouille sausage, diced
½	Tablespoon shallots, diced
3	Tablespoons butter
½	Tablespoon chicken base
½	Tablespoon lobster base
5	cups water
2	cups stone ground grits
2	cups heavy cream
¾	ounce Tabasco sauce
6	ounces Havarti cheese, shredded
¾	cup parmesan cheese, grated
6	ounces precooked crawfish, chopped
24	large grilled Florida shrimp, peeled, deveined with tail on

Directions

1. Sauté sausage and shallots in butter in a large stock pot.
2. Add chicken base, lobster base and water and bring to boil.
3. Add grits and heavy cream; simmer until reduced, 20 to 30 minutes, stirring often.
4. Add Tabasco sauce, Havarti cheese and Parmesan cheese; simmer and stir constantly until cheese is melted and grits are tender.
5. Fold in crawfish; cook for another 5 minutes, stirring constantly.
6. Scoop 6 ounces of grits into center of plate and top each serving with 3 large grilled shrimp.
7. Garnish with roasted red pepper sauce (see recipe on page 35).

Chef's tip

For an hors d'oeuvre size serving, place a small scoop of grits in center of plate and top with one shrimp for a perfect starter.

Crawfish are also called crayfish or crawdads. They are freshwater crustaceans resembling small lobsters, to which they are related. Crawfish are available frozen in most grocery stores.

Photo by John Sluder

Soups

Chicken Velvet Soup

Makes 12 servings

Ingredients

1½	sticks butter
¾	cup flour
1	cup warm milk
6	cups hot chicken stock
1	cup warm cream
1½	cups cooked chicken meat, chopped
	Kosher salt and white pepper to taste.

Directions

1. Make a blond roux with butter and flour by heating butter in stock pot and stirring in flour.
2. Sauté until beige in color and flour has cooked.
3. Add warm milk a small amount at a time, stirring until lump free after each addition.
4. Add chicken stock in the same manner until it becomes incorporated and lump free and resembles a thick gravy.
5. Add cream and chicken meat and simmer for 15 to 20 minutes, stirring periodically.

Cream of Tomato Soup

Makes 16 one-cup servings

Ingredients

½	pound butter
2	cups yellow onions, diced ¼ inch thick
2	cups celery, diced 1/4"
1	12-ounce can tomato paste
3	large fresh tomatoes, cored, chopped
5	cups half and half
12	cups chicken or vegetable stock
1	cup cornstarch
2	cups water

Directions

1. Cook onions and celery in butter until onions are clear.
2. Add tomato paste, tomatoes, sugar, water, and stock.
3. Bring to a boil.
4. Add cornstarch to water to make a slurry.
5. Whisk slurry into soup while its boiling.
6. Turn down and simmer for 10 minutes before serving.

Hearty Vegetable Bean Soup

Makes 10 one-cup servings

Ingredients

- 3 carrots, chopped
- 3 large onions, chopped
- 4 celery stalks, chopped
- 2 cups kidney beans, cooked
- 2 cups butter beans, cooked
- 8 ounces broccoli, chopped
- 5 cups beef stock or 5 cups water and 5 to 6 beef bouillon cubes according to taste

Directions

1. Sauté carrots, onions and celery in a small amount of oil (olive or canola).
2. Add beef stock to vegetables.
3. Add cooked or canned kidney beans and butter beans.
4. Bring to boil, then simmer on low heat for 30 minutes.
5. Add broccoli and simmer for 5 to 10 minutes.
6. Serve with Stuart's herb bread.

Nancy's Onion Soup
Makes 8 one-cup servings

Ingredients

14-18	red onions, thinly sliced in circles
¼	cup olive oil
4	Tablespoons butter
2	Tablespoons sugar
	Salt and pepper to taste
8	cups beef broth
4	slices bread
4	slices mozzarella cheese

Directions

1. Preheat oven to 350° F.
2. Cook onions in olive oil.
3. When onions are clear, add butter, salt, pepper, sugar, and beef broth.
4. Stir well.
5. Pour into large baking dish.
6. Top with bread and cheese.
7. Bake in 350° F oven for 15 minutes.
8. Serve hot.

May be prepared in individual baking dishes as pictured below.

Cream of Mushroom Soup
Makes 12 one-cup servings

Ingredients

5	portobello mushrooms, sliced
1	pound butter
½	pound all purpose flour
1	carrot, diced
2	celery sticks, diced
½	yellow onion, diced
1	Tablespoon parsley
3	Tablespoons chicken base
1	quart heavy cream
1	quart milk
1	quart water
	Salt and pepper to taste

Directions

1. Sauté mushrooms, carrots, celery, parsley and onions in butter.
2. When vegetables are tender, add flour and stir to form a roux.
3. Stir roux for about 4 minutes until flour is cooked.
4. Add chicken base and water a half cup at a time; stir until lump free between each addition.
5. Repeat process with milk and heavy cream.
6. Bring to a boil and serve.

Manhattan Clam Chowder

Makes 8 one-cup servings

Ingredients

20	chowder clams, washed or three 6-ounce cans chopped clams
5	cups water
2	large potatoes, medium diced
6	strips bacon, minced
2	cups onions, medium diced
2	medium carrots, diced
2	stalks celery, sliced ½ inch thick
1	leek, white only, medium diced
1	green pepper, medium diced
1	teaspoon garlic, mashed into paste
2	cups tomato, seeded and coarsely chopped
½	teaspoons dried oregano
	Salt, white pepper, Tabasco, Worcestershire sauce to taste

Directions

1. Steam the clams in water in a covered pot until they open.
2. Pick, chop, and reserve the clams. Strain and reserve the clam broth.
3. If using canned clams, drain and reserve broth.
4. Sauté bacon on low heat to extract the fat in a soup pot.
5. Sauté in the rendered bacon on low heat onions, carrots, celery, leeks and green peppers.
6. Add garlic; sauté until an aroma is apparent.
7. Add the diced tomatoes, oregano, clam broth and potatoes.
8. Simmer 30 minutes.
9. Degrease (skim any fat from the top) the soup and add clams.
10. Adjust the seasoning to taste with salt, white pepper, Tabasco and Worcestershire sauce.

BLACK BEAN SOUP

Makes 8 one-cup servings

Ingredients

1	carrot, diced
1	onion, diced
2	celery sticks, diced
1	green pepper, diced
2	tomatoes, diced
1	Tablespoon fresh garlic, diced
1	Tablespoon scallions, sliced
2	Tablespoons tomato paste
2	Tablespoons chicken bullion
1	teaspoon cayenne pepper
1	teaspoon cumin seed
5	cups water
2	one-pound cans black beans, rinsed and drained
	Sour cream for garnish

Directions

1. Sauté first seven ingredients in a small amount of oil in stock pot.
2. Once vegetables are tender, add water and remaining ingredients.
3. Simmer for 30 minutes.
4. Remove half the soup, place in blender and puree until smooth.
5. Return puree to pot and stir.
6. Bring back to a boil, remove from heat and serve topped with sour cream.

EGGPLANT STEW

Makes 12 one-cup servings

Ingredients

4	potatoes, peeled and cut into cubes
2	medium eggplants, peeled and cut into cubes
1	hard squash, peeled and cut into cubes
1	large onion, chopped
4	carrots, sliced ½-inch thick
1	35-ounce can peeled plum tomatoes
1	Tablespoon garam masala (page 28)
	Salt and pepper to taste

Directions

1. Sauté meat and onion in a small amount of olive oil.
2. Mix all ingredients together in large bowl and pour into a casserole dish.
3. Cover and bake at 400° F for 1 hour or until meat and potatoes are tender.

This stew is so thick, it may be used as a side dish.

Soups

Strawberry Gazpacho topped with Jicama Salad

Makes 24 cups

Soup Ingredients

6	pounds fresh California strawberries, stemmed and chopped
2¼	pounds plum tomatoes, chopped
1½	pounds English cucumber, peeled, seeded and chopped
9	cloves garlic
3	jalapeño peppers
1½	cups sherry vinegar
	Salt and black pepper as needed.

Directions

1. In blender, purée strawberries, tomatoes, cucumbers, garlic, jalapeños and vinegar.
2. Season with salt and pepper and chill.

Jicama Salad   Makes 8 cups

Ingredients

8	cups jicama, peeled and julienned
2	bunches chives, cut in 1½-inch lengths
6	Tablespoons extra virgin olive oil
3	Tablespoons fresh thyme leaves
	Salt and pepper as needed.
1½	pounds goat cheese

Directions

1. Combine jicama, chives, oil and thyme; season with salt and pepper.
2. For each serving, mound 1/3 cup jicama salad in center of soup plate.
3. Carefully ladle 1 cup strawberry gazpacho around salad.
4. Top with 1 ounce goat cheese, formed into a ball.

Recipe and photograph provided courtesy of the California Strawberry Commission © 2009 California Strawberry Commission. All rights reserved.

Caldo Gallego

Makes 16 one-cup servings

Photo courtesy of Melissa Camero Ainslie

Ingredients

1	pound white beans
¼	cup olive oil
½	pound lean salt pork, chopped into ¼ inch cubes
½	cup chopped, cooked ham
½	pound sliced chorizo sausage
2	hard tomatoes, peeled and chopped
6-8	garlic cloves, crushed
1	ham bone, pork hock or neck bones
3	quarts water
4-6	small white potatoes or turnips, peeled and chopped
1	pound chopped spinach or collard greens (preferred)

Directions

1. Cover beans with water and soak overnight.
2. Discard water.
3. Draw fat out of salt pork by sautéing in olive oil in a large pot or skillet.
4. Add ham and sausage and cook until slightly browned.
5. Add tomatoes and garlic and continue cooking for a few minutes.
6. Add beans, ham bone and water.
7. Bring to a boil, then simmer for 3 hours.
8. During the last hour add potatoes or turnips.
9. During the last 30 minutes add the spinach or collard greens.

Chef's tip

This recipe was given to me by my friend Luis Martinez of the Cocoa Beach Daybreak Rotary Club. Caldo is Spanish for soup and this recipe is from Galicia or the Gallego part of Spain. Many cafes and gas stations keep a pot going over a fire all year and add ingredients as they come into season. Luis suggests this recipe be made a few days in advance and then reheated for serving.

Soups

Pumpkin Soup

Makes 8 - 10 one-cup servings

Ingredients

½	small onion, chopped
½	cup celery, chopped
2	Tablespoons butter
3	cups pumpkin, cooked and mashed
5	cups chicken broth
1	teaspoon salt
	pepper to taste
2	bay leaves
½	teaspoon thyme, crushed
1	Tablespoon brown sugar
1-2	cups heavy cream, according to desired taste and consistency
¼	teaspoon nutmeg
½	teaspoon cinnamon
	Sour cream for garnish
	Chopped chives for garnish

Directions

1. In Dutch oven, sauté onion and celery in butter until tender, about 5 to 10 minutes.
2. Add pumpkin, broth, salt, pepper, bay leaves, thyme and sugar.
3. Bring to boil, reduce heat and simmer for 30 minutes.
4. Remove and discard bay leaves.
5. Add cream a little at a time, to desired consistency. (For a low fat soup, replace heavy cream with nonfat or skim milk.)
6. Stir in cinnamon and nutmeg.
7. Heat to serving temperature but do not boil.
8. Before serving, top with sour cream and sprinkle with chives.

SALADS

Tropical Macaroni Salad

Makes 10 one-cup servings

Ingredients

5	cups cooked (2½ cups uncooked) tricolor rotini, prepared according to package directions, rinsed, drained and chilled
1½	cup mayonnaise or coconut yogurt
¼	cup red onion, finely chopped
¼	cup grated carrots
½	cup green bell pepper, finely diced
1	cup grape tomatoes, quartered
1	cup seedless red grapes, quartered
1	cup mandarin oranges, drained
1	cup pineapple tidbits, drained
1	fresh squeezed lemon or lime
	Salt and pepper to taste

Directions

1. Boil macaroni according to directions; rinse and chill.
2. Combine prepared red onion, carrots, green pepper, tomatoes, grapes, oranges and pineapple tidbits in large bowl and toss.
3. Stir 1 cup mayonnaise or coconut yogurt into the vegetable/fruit mix.
4. Stir chilled macaroni into vegetable/fruit mix.
5. Toss to combine thoroughly.
6. Add salt, pepper, and/or citrus juice to taste.
7. Chill in refrigerator for several hours.
8. Just before serving, stir in remaining chilled mayonnaise or coconut yogurt to reach desired consistency.

Yellow Dog Macaroni Salad

Makes 12 servings

Ingredients

1	16-ounce box macaroni
1	green pepper, chopped
½	red onion, chopped
½	carrot, grated
2	cups mayonnaise
1	cup sugar
2	Tablespoons apple cider vinegar
1	Tablespoon parsley flakes
	Salt and pepper to taste

Directions

1. Boil macaroni according to directions, drain and cool.
2. In large bowl, combine macaroni, green pepper, onion and carrots with mayonnaise, sugar, and vinegar.
3. Salt and pepper to taste.
4. Chill before serving.

Phil's Famous Potato Salad

Makes 12 servings

Ingredients

5	pounds red potatoes
6	hard boiled eggs
1	onion, finely chopped
1	4-ounce jar diced pimentos, drained
½	cup sweet relish, drained
1	Tablespoon brown mustard
1	cup Miracle Whip Light
	Salt and pepper to taste
	Fresh parsley and paprika for garnish.

Chef's note

Contributed by my friend Phil Crews, my editor's husband, who cooks this for large groups on the Space Coast.

Directions

1. Boil potatoes in skins until done (to test, pierce largest with knife).
2. Drain, cool, then remove skins and cut potatoes into ¾ - inch cubes.
3. Boil eggs for 8 minutes. Cool, peel and chop.
4. In large bowl, combine chopped potatoes, eggs, drained pimentos sweet relish, mustard and Miracle Whip Light until well blended.
5. Add salt and pepper to taste.
6. Place in serving dish, sprinkle with paprika and arrange parsley sprigs for garnish.
7. Chill at least one hour before serving.

Yellow Dog Coleslaw
Makes 12 servings

Ingredients

1	head green cabbage, shredded
1	green pepper, chopped
½	red onion, chopped
½	carrot, grated

Sauce

2	cups mayonnaise
1	cup sugar
2	Tablespoons apple cider vinegar
1	Tablespoon parsley flakes
	Salt and pepper to taste

Directions

1. Thinly shred cabbage with a sharp knife or mandolin.
2. Chop onion and pepper into small pieces and place in food processor.
3. Pulse into fine pieces. Add to cabbage.
4. Grate carrots and add to cabbage.
5. Add remaining ingredients and mix until well incorporated.
6. Let rest in refrigerator 1 to 2 hours before serving.
7. Toss again before serving.

Blueberry Spinach Salad

Makes one serving

Ingredients

- 3/4 cup fresh baby spinach leaves, washed
- 2 Tablespoons bleu cheese plus extra for garnish
- 1 Tablespoon chopped pecans plus extra for garnish
- ¼ cup fresh blueberries
- 3 Tablespoons balsamic vinaigrette

Directions

1. Put spinach in a large bowl.
2. Add all ingredients and toss.
3. Top with extra bleu cheese and pecans.
4. Serve immediately.

Salads

Copper Penny Salad

Makes 12 servings

Ingredients

- 2 pounds carrots, sliced to thickness of a penny
- 1 medium green pepper, sliced in strips
- 1 medium onion, cut in rings
- 1 10-ounce can condensed tomato soup
- ½ cup canola oil
- 1 cup sugar
- ¾ cup rice vinegar or apple cider vinegar
- 1 teaspoon Worcestershire sauce
- 1 teaspoon salt
- ½ teaspoon pepper
- 1 teaspoon mustard powder

Photo by John Sluder

Directions

1. Slice raw carrots into circles the thickness of a penny.
2. Cover with water and cook until just barely tender (five minutes or so after coming to a boil).
3. Drain, rinse and cool.
4. Cut onion and green pepper into rings or slices and add to carrots.
5. Combine remaining ingredients and mix well.
6. Pour mixture over combined carrots, onion and green pepper.
7. Toss until completely covered. Store in sealed plastic container.
8. Refrigerate over night, flipping container upside down half way through.
9. Serve cold.
10. Keeps up to 2 weeks in refrigerator.

91

Sandwiches

Top Dog

Makes one servings

Ingredients

¾	cup tuna salad (see recipe below)
¼	cup romaine lettuce, sliced thin
1	slice tomato
1	slice bacon, fried
1	slice Havarti cheese
1	slice dill pickle
1	bread roll, sliced lengthwise

Tuna salad

1	5-ounce can tuna
2	olives, chopped
1	picante pepper, sliced
1	Tablespoon red onion, finely chopped
1	Tablespoon celery, finely chopped
3	Tablespoons mayonnaise
	Salt and pepper to taste

Directions

1. Mix tuna with olives, peppers, onion, celery and mayonnaise.
2. Salt and pepper to taste and blend well.
3. Spread tuna salad on bottom of bread roll.
4. Top with lettuce, tomato, bacon and cheese.
5. Close with top of bread roll.
6. Serve with pickle on the side.

Lady Dog

Makes 1 vegetarian serving

Ingredients

1	Portobello mushroom, grilled or baked
½	roasted red pepper
1	artichoke heart, chopped
¼	cup fresh spinach, chopped
1	slice Havarti cheese (optional)
1	Tablespoon balsamic salad dressing
2	slices focaccia bread or toasted bun

Directions

1. Grill or bake mushroom to desired doneness.
2. Toast or grill both slices focaccia bread.
3. Place sliced Portobello mushroom on bottom of bun.
4. Top with artichoke and spinach and drizzle with small amount of balsamic dressing.
5. Top with sliced roasted red pepper and cheese if desired.
6. Place under broiler for 2 to 3 minutes or until the cheese melts; or place in oven at 350° F for 5 minutes.
7. Remove from oven, add top half of bun and serve.

Sandwiches

THE YELLOW DOG FAVORITE

Makes 1 serving

Ingredients

1	medium portobello mushroom, grilled and sliced
¼	roasted red pepper, chopped
1	slice Havarti cheese
2	slices focaccia bread, toasted
1	patty grilled beef, chicken or fish

Directions

1. Grill meat over flame.
2. Meanwhile, sauté mushroom slices or grill whole mushroom with meat, then slice.
3. Place meat on one piece of toasted focaccia bread and top with Havarti cheese.
4. Top with roasted red peppers and remaining slice of bread.
5. Serve hot.

In memory of Deputy Officer Tinio

For her birthday, Nancy Tinio Borton purchased a police dog for the Brevard County, Florida Sheriff's department. The German shepherd took Nancy's maiden name. After distinguished service, he retired and lived out his life in leisure.

Yellow Dog Café ™ Cookbook

Good Ole Dog

Makes 1 serving

Ingredients

- ¼ cup onion, sliced
- 1 8-ounce beef patty
- 2 slices fresh tomato
- ¼ cup shredded romaine lettuce
- 1 sandwich roll, sliced lengthwise

Directions:

1. Sauté onions in 1 teaspoon oil until caramelized.
2. Grill beef patty.
3. Place lettuce and tomato on the sandwich roll.
4. Top with beef patty and caramelized onion.
5. Add a slice of your favorite cheese, if desired and serve.

Sandwiches

THE CALIFORNIA DREAMER
Makes 1 serving

Ingredients

1	patty of grilled beef, chicken or fish
3	slices Brie cheese
2	slices tomato
¼	cup alfalfa sprouts
2	teaspoons fresh chopped scallions
1	Tablespoon guacamole (see recipe below)
1	Tablespoon salsa (see page 42)
2	slices focaccia bread
1	pickle

Directions

1. Grill beef, chicken or fish.
2. Toast focaccia bread
3. Top one slice of bread with meat and brie cheese.
4. Broil until cheese is soft.
5. Top with tomato, alfalfa sprouts, scallions, guacamole and salsa.
6. Close with remaining slice of bread.

QUICK AND EASY GUACAMOLE
Serves 8

Ingredients

4	ripe avocados, mashed
2	cloves garlic, crushed
	Juice of half a lemon
1	jalapeño pepper, seeded and chopped
½	red onion, finely chopped
1	large ripe tomato, chopped
8-10	sprigs fresh cilantro, minced
	Freshly ground sea salt to taste.

Directions

1. Combine mashed avocados with crushed garlic and juice of half a lemon, stirring until smooth
2. Add remaining ingredients, blending well, adjusting the salt to taste.

Contributed by Alyssa Hickson

Shrimp Salad Sandwich

Makes 4 servings

Ingredients

- 1 pound cooked shrimp
- 2 Tablespoons mayonnaise
- 2 Tablespoons ketchup
- 2 Tablespoons whole grain or Dijon mustard
- 1 cup celery, sliced
- 2 Tablespoons red pepper, diced into ¼-inch cubes
- 2 Tablespoons red onion, diced into ¼-inch cubes
- 1 teaspoon parsley, chopped
- Pinch cayenne pepper
- Pinch salt
- Pinch Old Bay seasoning
- Juice of one lemon
- 4 baguettes

Directions

1. Peel shrimp and cut in half lengthwise, removing the back vein. Set aside.
2. Mix remaining ingredients together, then fold in shrimp.
3. Cut baguettes in half, top with shrimp salad and serve.

Chef's tip

This also makes a nice salad served on a bed of lettuce, as pictured.

Sandwiches

Stuffed Hamburgers
Makes 4 servings

Ingredients

2	pounds ground chuck
2	eggs
½	cup breadcrumbs
1½	teaspoons salt
¼	teaspoon pepper
½	pound mushrooms, chopped (2 cups)
1	Tablespoon butter
½	cup shredded sharp cheese
1	large onion, sliced
1	sandwich roll

Directions

1. Combine beef, eggs, breadcrumbs, salt and pepper, mixing well.
2. Divide into 8 thin patties.
3. Sauté onions in butter until golden.
4. Add mushrooms and continue sautéing until caramelized.
5. Spoon onion/mushroom mixture on center of four patties.
6. Top each of the 4 patties with 2 Tablespoons cheese.
7. Arrange one plain patty over a cheese topped patty, pressing edges to seal. (This gives four stuffed patties.)
8. Cook in frying pan for 5 to 8 minutes, turning once.
9. Place between two slices of the sandwich roll or bread of your choice.

Chef's tip

Instead of making a sandwich with the patties, fry them, then top with beef gravy for a tasty entree.

Sides

Cilantro Rice

Makes 8 servings

Ingredients

2	cups rice
	Salt and pepper to taste
1	cup onion, chopped
1	clove garlic, chopped
4	cups chicken stock
1	cup blanched spinach
5	stems cilantro, chopped
1	Tablespoon oil

Directions

1. In stock pot, sauté garlic, onion and cilantro in oil until onions are tender.
2. Add rice and chicken stock and bring to a boil.
3. Reduce heat to a simmer, cover and cook for 15 minutes.
4. Add spinach and cook covered another five minutes or until rice is tender.

Wild Rice Grilled Vegetable Griddle Cakes

Makes 24 four-inch cakes

Ingredients

2	cups grilled vegetables, chopped
2	cups cooked wild rice
4	egg whites, whipped stiff
2	eggs
½	Tablespoon baking powder
1	teaspoon baking soda
1¾	cups flour
1½	cups half and half
1	teaspoon tarragon
	Salt and pepper to taste

Directions

1. Separate egg whites and whip until stiff; set yolks aside.
2. Blend dry ingredients together in large bowl.
3. Add half and half and egg yolks; mix well.
4. Stir in rice and vegetables, then carefully fold in whipped egg whites.
5. Carefully ladle ½ cup batter into a heated sauté pan coated with oil.
6. Cook until golden brown, about one minute on each side or until done.
7. Serve hot.

Wild Rice

Makes 2 servings

Ingredients

1	cup wild rice
2½	cups chicken stock
¼	cup sherry
	Salt and pepper to taste

Directions

1. In a 2-quart sauce pan, combine all ingredients.
2. Bring to a boil, reduce heat to a simmer and cover with a lid.
3. Cook until rice is tender (about 30 minutes).

Sides

Pommes Anna

Makes 4 servings

Ingredients

2½ pounds potatoes
1 stick butter
Salt and pepper to taste

Directions

1. Preheat oven to 375° F.
2. Peel and slice potatoes very thin and place one layer in shallow dish or 9-inch pie plate.
3. Cut thin slices of butter across first layer and sprinkle with salt and pepper.
4. Repeat with remaining potatoes, ending with butter on top.
5. Tightly cover with foil and weight the top with a heavy cast iron skillet.
6. Bake at 375° F for 30 minutes or until the potato pie is brown and crisp on the outside and soft and buttery on the inside.
7. Invert onto serving plate.
8. Cut into 4 wedges to serve.

Spinach Souffle

Makes 6 servings

Ingredients

- 3 cups tightly packed fresh spinach leaves, coarsely chopped, steamed and drained
- 2 egg yolks
- ¼ cup grated Romano cheese
- Dash of ground nutmeg
- 4 egg whites
- ¼ teaspoon cream of tartar
- 3 Tablespoons grated Parmesan cheese
- 1 Tablespoon butter

Directions

1. Preheat oven to 325° F.
2. In food processor, combine steamed and drained spinach with egg yolks; process on medium speed until smooth, scraping down the sides as necessary.
3. Transfer to a large mixing bowl.
4. Stir in the Romano cheese and a dash of ground nutmeg.
5. In a separate bowl, with mixer, beat egg whites until they form stiff peaks.
6. Stir one quarter of the egg whites into the spinach and egg yolk mixture, then gently fold in the remaining egg whites.
7. Lightly grease a 2-quart souffle dish with butter and sprinkle with Parmesan cheese.
8. Gently pour the spinach mixture into the souffle dish or 6 small ramekin dishes as pictured.
9. Bake at 325° F for 30 minutes (10 to 12 minutes if using ramekins). (Resist the temptation to open oven for a peek as souffles are delicate and will fall!)
10. Remove from oven with care and serve immediately.

Yellow Dog Stuffing

Makes 8 servings

Ingredients

5	sticks celery, diced
1	medium onion, diced
8-10	cups diced bread
1	stick butter
2	Tablespoons house spice mix (see page 26)
2	cups chicken stock
2	eggs

Directions

1. In large heavy bottomed pot, sauté onions and celery in butter and spice mix until onions are translucent.
2. Whip eggs and chicken stock together.
3. Add to sautéed onions and celery.
4. Quickly fold in about 8 cups of bread.
5. Continue cooking on stove top until mixture starts to stick to bottom of pan.
6. If mixture is too wet, add more bread and continue to brown, folding crusted bottom into the mixture.
7. Cook about 5 to 10 minutes longer, continuing to fold mixture until done.

Fried Onions

Makes 12 cups onion rings

Ingredients

- 2 large red onions, sliced thin on a mandolin
- 1 cup Stuart's dry fry mix (see page 54)
- 1 teaspoon cayenne pepper
- Salt and pepper to taste

Directions

1. Slice red onions paper thin.
2. Toss in dry fry mix seasoned with cayenne, pepper and salt.
3. Fry in deep fryer in small batches until crisp.
4. Drain on paper towels.

Chef's tip

These onion rings are great as a side dish or may be chopped and used as a topping for various casseroles or as a crust for meat, such as onion crusted chicken, grouper or mahi mahi (see page 151).

Potato Cakes

Makes 12 cakes

Ingredients

- 4 cups cooked mashed potatoes, cold
- 1 cup grated parmesan cheese
- 3 cups Stuart's dry fry mix (page 54)
- ½ cup water
- 1 cup Panko bread crumbs
- 1 teaspoon cayenne pepper
- 1-2 cups canola oil
- Salt and pepper to taste

Directions

1. Warm mashed potatoes in microwave and fold in cheese.
2. Form mixture into 4-inch patties.
3. Combine 1 cup dry fry mix with cayenne pepper, black pepper and salt; set aside.
4. Coat patties with seasoned mix.
5. Mix remaining 2 cups of Stuart's dry fry mix with enough water to make dipping easy.
6. Dip each coated patty into batter, then roll in Panko.
7. Fry in small batches in ½-inch canola oil in pan until crisp on both sides.
8. Drain on paper towels and serve hot.

Potato Puffs

Makes 16 to 24 balls

Ingredients

- 4 cups cooked mashed potatoes, cold
- 2 cups Stuart's dry fry mix (page 54)
- ½ cup water
- Canola oil for frying

Directions

1. Heat deep fryer to 350° F or large heavy bottom pot with 3 inches oil.
2. Form cold mashed potatoes into 2-inch round balls.
3. Toss in dry fry mix and set balls aside.
4. Mix left over fry mix with just enough water to make dipping easy.
5. Dip each coated ball in wet mix and fry in small batches until crisp.
6. Drain on paper towels; serve hot, as pictured below.

Chayote Succotash

Makes 8 one-cup servings

Ingredients

5	chayote squash
1	large onion
2	red bell peppers
2	cups frozen corn
1½	cups frozen peas
1	chipotle pepper, rinsed and seeded
1½	cups heavy cream
1	cup water
1½	Tablespoons chicken base
1	stick butter
1	lime

Directions

1. Slice chayote in half, remove seeds, coat with oil and season with salt and pepper.
2. Roast at 350° F for 30 minutes.
3. While chayote is roasting, roughly dice onions and bell pepper and mince the chipotle.
4. After chayote cools, trim off stem end and dice into large pieces.
5. In large pot, sauté in butter the onions and bell pepper for 7 minutes.
6. Add chayote and cook for 10 minutes more.
7. Add corn, peas, chipotle and water with chicken base.
8. Cook down for 10 to 15 minutes at a low boil, seasoning with salt and pepper to taste.
9. Finish with squeeze of lime and a touch of butter and serve.

Chayote squash is also known as a vegetable pear or pear squash that belongs to the gourd family along with melons, cucumbers and squash. It may be eaten raw or cooked.

Sides

Stuart's Delmonico Potatoes

Makes 4 - 6 servings

Ingredients

5	medium Russet or Yukon gold potatoes
1	cup half and half
½	teaspoon salt
¼	teaspoon white pepper
¼	teaspoon grated or ground nutmeg
4	Tablespoons Parmesan cheese, finely grated
3	Tablespoons butter

Directions

1. Scrub potatoes well, and with skins on, quarter lengthwise and rinse.
2. Place potatoes in saucepan and cover with water.
3. Bring to boil and simmer for no more than 10 minutes (you do not want them to fully cook).
4. Drain and submerse potatoes in cold water, allowing to cool at least a half hour.
5. Preheat oven to 425° F.
6. Meanwhile, grate potatoes into long strips.
7. In a mixing bowl, combine half and half, salt, white pepper and nutmeg.
8. Preheat a large frying pan over medium heat and add half the butter, potatoes and half and half mixture, folding together gently without mashing the potatoes.
9. Cook for 10 minutes, mixing gently a few times. Do not allow to burn.
10. Remove potatoes from stove and fold in 2 tablespoons grated Parmesan.
11. Transfer potatoes into a pre-buttered baking dish and arrange evenly.
12. Bake uncovered for 6 to 7 minutes or until lightly browned.
13. Top with remaining Parmesan cheese and serve immediately.

Tuna Tataki

Serves 2

Ingredients

1. 8-ounce tuna steak
2. Tablespoons fresh grated ginger
½ cup soy sauce

Directions

1. Mix grated ginger with soy sauce and set aside to marinade.
2. Sear tuna on each side on a very hot grill.
3. Slice thinly and arrange on plate.
4. Top with strained ginger marinade.
5. Garnish with pickled ginger and seaweed salad and wasabi.

Appetizers

111

Photo by John Sluder

Pistachio Crusted Tuna Skewers

Makes 6 skewers

Ingredients

4	Tablespoons Ponzu sauce (see recipe on page 32)
½	cup finely chopped pistachios, toasted
6	bamboo skewers, soaked in water for 10 minutes
1	pound tuna steak, cut into 18 1-inch cubes

Directions

1. Preheat oven to 350° F.
2. Marinate tuna in Ponzu sauce for 15 minutes.
3. Press tuna into toasted, crushed pistachios until coated.
4. Thread three tuna squares onto each skewer.
5. Bake in oven for 3 minutes, turn, and bake an additional 3 minutes for medium well skewers (adjust baking time to your preference).
6. Serve with additional Ponzu sauce on the side.

Susan Hartgrave's Lobster Cheesecake

Makes 12 to 16 servings

Ingredients

1	cup freshly grated parmesan cheese
1	cup bread crumbs
½	cup melted butter
1	Tablespoon olive oil
1	cup chopped onions
½	cup chopped yellow bell peppers
½	cup chopped red bell peppers
2	teaspoons salt
1	teaspoon pepper
1¾	pounds cream cheese, softened
4	large eggs
½	cup heavy cream
1	cup grated smoked or regular gouda cheese
1	pound lobster meat, cooked and roughly chopped
½	cup chopped parsley
1	cup Crème Fraiche *(optional)*
1	Tablespoon finely chopped parsley leaves
7	ounces Ose tra caviar *(optional)*

Chef's note

Crème Fraiche is a soured cream containing butterfat. It can be made at home by adding a small amount of cultured buttermilk or sour cream to heavy cream, and allowing it to stand for several hours at room temperature until the bacterial cultures act on the cream.

Directions

1. Preheat oven to 350° F.
2. Combine parmesan cheese, bread crumbs and butter. Blend thoroughly then press the mixture into the bottom of a 9-inch pan.
3. In a large sauce pan, heat olive oil then add onions and peppers. Season with salt and pepper, sauté for 2 minutes then remove from heat.
4. Using an electric mixer, beat the cream cheese until smooth then add eggs one at a time while mixing, then add the cream, gouda cheese and sautéed peppers and onions until fully incorporated (about 2 minutes).
5. Fold in LOBSTER MEAT and parsley, then pour mixture into the prepared crust and bake until firm (about 1 hour).
6. Remove from oven and allow to cool to room temperature before serving.
7. If you refrigerate the dish before serving, allow it to come to room temperature before serving as well.
8. Cut the cheesecake into small wedges with a warm knife.
9. You may serve each wedge with the Crème Fraiche and caviar *(optional)*.

Caprese

Makes six servings

Ingredients

- 4 fresh tomatoes, sliced
- 1 pound buffalo Mozzarella, sliced
- ¼ cup extra virgin olive oil (or to taste)
- Salt and fresh ground pepper to taste
- Handful of fresh basil leaves
- Balsamic vinegar to taste.

Directions

1. Cut tomatoes into ½-inch thick slices.
2. Arrange desired amount of tomato slices on individual serving plates.
3. Top each tomato with a mozzarella slice and garnish with basil.
4. Drizzle with olive oil and balsamic vinegar.
5. Season with salt and pepper to taste.
6. Garnish with basil leaves and serve as an appetizer.

LAMB LOLLY POPS

Makes 4 appetizers or 2 servings as a meal

Ingredients

1   lamb rack, sliced between each bone
3   Tablespoons Stuart's lamb rub (page 27)
1   teaspoon dried or fresh chopped parsley
¼   cup malted mint sauce
     (See recipe on page 35)

Directions

1. Trim fat from the top of the chop.
2. Rinse each chop with water and pat dry with paper towel.
3. Rub chops with Stuart's lamb rub.
4. Grill chops about 2 minutes on each side until medium-rare.
5. Arrange crisscross on plate.
6. Garnish with parsley.
7. Serve with malted mint sauce on the side as an appetizer or as a meal with a rice dish.

Chef's tip

My favorite way to cook lamb chops is to grill them. Use a paring knife to scrape the bones before cooking so they look clean and can be used for a handle. Traditionally this dish is served with mint jelly.

Appetizers

Lamb Skewers

Makes 16 skewers

Ingredients

1	pound ground lamb meat
1	small onion, finely chopped
1	egg
1	Tablespoon chopped fresh parsley
	Salt and pepper to taste
16	4-inch skewers soaked in water

Directions

1. Mix meat with egg, onion, parsley, salt and pepper.
2. Add a little cold water to soften and mix by hand.
3. Separate meat mixture into 16 evenly sized balls.
4. Form balls into oblong shapes.
5. Thread one ball onto each skewer.
6. Broil to desired doneness and serve.

Chicken Crepes

Makes 4 servings

Ingredients

4	crepes (see page 55 for recipe)
8	ounces chicken breast, grilled and diced
¼	cup sliced blanched almonds
12	green seedless grapes, sliced in halves
8	spears asparagus, blanched and chopped
½	pound cream cheese
½	cup cheddar cheese, grated
¼	cup milk
	Salt and pepper to taste

Directions

1. Microwave cream cheese and milk, stirring every 30 seconds until incorporated.
2. Stir in remaining ingredients.
3. Microwave until it starts to bubble.
4. Spoon hot mixture along center of each crepe and roll or fold together, reserving ¼ cup cheese sauce for topping, adjusting the thickness by adding more milk. Sprinkle top with additional cheddar cheese.

Beef and Pineapple Skewers

Makes 3 servings

Ingredients

- 2 cups pineapple juice
- ¼ cup brown sugar
- 1 Tablespoon Dijon mustard
- 1/8 teaspoon salt
- 1/8 teaspoon pepper
- 1 teaspoon cooking oil
- ½ teaspoon garlic salt
- ¼ teaspoon pepper
- ½ pound beef tenderloin, cut into 12 cubes
- 12 pineapple chunks, 1 inch square
- 3 bamboo skewers, 8 inches long

Directions

1. Soak skewers in water for 10 minutes.
2. Combine pineapple juice and sugar in saucepan and simmer on medium heat until reduced to about ½ cup.
3. Stir in salt, pepper and mustard.
4. Add oil and garlic salt.
5. Toss beef in sauce, coating well.
6. Thread beef and pineapple onto soaked skewers.
7. Cook on greased grill on medium-high for about 6 minutes, or until they reach desired doneness, turning once and brushing with remaining sauce while still cooking.

Plantain Chips

With Mango Coconut Dip
Makes 4 servings

Photo by chef Billy Rose

Ingredients

- 2 large semi-ripe plantains, peeled
- 2 Tablespoons cooking oil
- 2 Tablespoons blackening spice mix (from recipe on page. 28)
- ¼ cup finely chopped ripe mango
- ¼ cup sour cream
- 2 Tablespoons coconut rum
- 2 Tablespoons medium sweetened coconut, toasted
- 1½ teaspoons granulated sugar
- 1½ teaspoons lime juice
- 1½ teaspoon ground allspice
- Pinch ground nutmeg

Directions

1. Cut plantains at a sharp angle into 1/8-inch thick slices.
2. Toss plantains in blackening spice mix.
3. Fry plantains in oil until crispy.
4. In separate bowl, combine mango, sour cream, rum, coconut, sugar, lime juice, allspice and nutmeg. Blend well.
5. Serve plantains with dip.

Appetizers

Leek and Mushroom Panzarotti

Makes 12 mini panzarotti

Ingredients

Dough
- 1 cup all-purpose flour
- 3 Tablespoons extra-virgin olive oil
- 1 pinch of salt
- 3 Tablespoons plus 1½ teaspoon water
- 1 teaspoon lard

Filling
- 2 Tablespoons duck fat or rendered bacon fat
- 1 small leek, rinsed and thinly sliced
- 1½ ounces Panko (Japanese style) bread crumbs
- 1/3 cup milk
- 1 Tablespoon truffle oil
- 2 cups assorted mixed mushrooms, sliced
- Sunflower oil for frying

 Chef's tip

You may also use the basic meat pie dough on page 47. Make dough as directed; divide into 1-inch round balls, let proof. When doubled in size, press down with fingers until very thin, spoon leek and mushroom mixture onto one half, and egg wash the edges so dough sticks when folded. Press closed with tines of fork and fry in hot oil, turning once.

Directions

1. Pour flour into bowl and add the olive oil, salt, water, and lard.
2. Mix thoroughly, then transfer to work surface and knead until the dough is smooth and elastic.
3. Wrap in plastic wrap and refrigerate for ½ hour.
4. Heat the butter in a frying pan and sauté the leek and mushrooms, adding a little water if necessary, until the leeks are translucent and the mushrooms tender.
5. Soak the Panko in the milk until soft, then drain and squeeze out excess liquid.
6. Mix together the soaked bread crumbs, sautéed leek and mushrooms, and truffle oil. Season to taste with salt and pepper.
7. Roll out the dough and cut into 4-inch circles.
8. Place 1 Tablespoon leek and mushroom mixture on half the circle, fold over and seal the edges.
9. Heat the sunflower oil until very hot, then fry the stuffed dough until golden.

Photo by John Sluder

Pineapple Ceviche
Makes 4 servings

Ingredients

- 12 ounces grouper, wahoo, sea bass or snapper, diced in ¼ to ½-inch pieces
- 1/3 cup fresh lime juice
- ½ cup pineapple juice
- 1½ Tablespoons serrano pepper, diced
- 1½ Tablespoons red bell pepper, diced
- 2 Tablespoons yellow pepper, diced
- 1½ Tablespoons red onion, diced
- 1 teaspoon minced garlic
- 2 Tablespoons chopped cilantro
- 1 Tablespoon olive oil
- Salt & Pepper to taste

Directions

1. Combine all ingredients and chill in refrigerator for at least 4 hours.
2. Serve chilled and garnish with lime wedges and plantain chips (page 117).

Appetizers

Olive Tapenade

Makes 1¼ cup

Ingredients

1	cup assorted olives
½	teaspoon garlic
1	Tablespoon shallots
1	teaspoon Dijon mustard
1	teaspoon fresh lemon juice
	Salt and Pepper to taste
¼	cup capers, rinsed
3	anchovy filets
½	Tablespoon fresh rosemary

Directions

1. Finely dice olives
2. Blend remaining ingredients in food processor.
3. Fold olives into paste.
4. Season to taste with salt and pepper.
5. Serve as a spread for bread or crackers.
6. Also use in place of butter or as a topping for many meat and fish dishes.

Tapenade Toasts

Makes 8 canapes

Ingredients

8	baguette bread slices, less than ½ inch thick
1	Tablespoon olive oil
¼	cup soft goat cheese (Chevre)
½	cup olive tapenade (see recipe above).
1	Tablespoon thinly sliced fresh basil

Directions

1. Preheat oven to 350° F.
2. Arrange bread slices on a baking sheet.
3. Brush with olive oil. Bake for 5 to 7 minutes until golden brown.
4. Turn over and brush with olive oil.
5. Bake until golden and crisp.
6. Spread with goat cheese and top with a Tablespoon of tapenade.
7. Sprinkle with basil and serve.

Spicy Sesame Vegetable Skewers

Makes 12

Ingredients

1	pint cherry tomatoes
2	yellow squash, cut into 1 X 2 inch pieces, removing seeds
2	zucchinis, cut into 1 X 2 inch pieces, removing seeds
1/3	cup sesame oil
½	cup crushed red pepper flakes
2	teaspoons finely grated ginger root
2	teaspoons granulated sugar
½	teaspoon salt
12	6-inch bamboo skewers, soaked in water for 10 minutes

Directions

1. Thread first 3 ingredients onto skewers, starting with zucchini, then alternating a tomato, squash, second tomato, and zucchini.
2. Combine remaining ingredients and blend well.
3. Brush vegetable skewers lightly with sesame oil mixture.
4. Cook skewers on a greased grill, brushing occasionally with sesame oil mixture until vegetables are tender.
5. Remove from grill, brush with remaining sesame oil mixture and transfer to a serving plate.

Carrot Patties

Makes 15 to 20 patties

Ingredients

1	cup shredded carrots
½	cup tempura batter (see recipe on page 53)
½	cup golden raisins

Directions

1. Fold raisins and carrots into tempura batter.
2. Drop by heaping tablespoon into a hot oiled sauté pan; spread flat with a spoon.
3. Cook each side until golden brown, turning once.
4. Serve immediately with your favorite dipping sauce as an appetizer or as a side dish with your entree.

Appetizers

Polenta Squares with Spicy Shrimp Ragout

Makes 12 canapés

Ingredients

Polenta Squares
- 2 cups water with a dash salt
- 1 cup instant polenta
- sunflower oil for frying

Spicy Shrimp
- ¼ pound butter
- 1 Tablespoon minced garlic
- 1 Tablespoon chopped shallots
- 1 onion, chopped
- ½ red bell pepper, chopped
- ½ green bell pepper, chopped
- ¼ cup chopped celery
- 1 large tomato, diced
- 1 Tablespoon tomato paste
- 1 Tablespoon sugar
- 1 Tablespoon crushed red pepper
- 1 Tablespoon blackening spice (see page 28)
- 12 large shrimp, sliced lengthwise
- salt and pepper to taste

Directions

Polenta squares
1. Salt the water, bring to boil, and slowly stir in the polenta.
2. Continue stirring for 5 minutes.
3. Line a bread pan with wax paper or plastic wrap and add polenta.
4. Let cool and refrigerate until firm.

Spicy shrimp ragout
5. Sauté garlic, onions and shallots in butter until soft.
6. Add remaining chopped vegetables, sugar, tomato paste and spices.
7. Simmer on medium heat for 20 minutes. Add salt and pepper to taste.
8. Add shrimp and simmer for another 10 minutes.
9. Remove cooled polenta from pan and cut into slices.
10. Fry the polenta in the sunflower oil until golden brown, drain, and dry on paper towels.
11. Top the crunchy polenta with the ragout, placing two slices of shrimp on top of each canapé and serve immediately.

Crab Cakes

Makes 9 cakes

Ingredients

3	Tablespoons mayonnaise
1	teaspoon Old Bay seasoning
½	Tablespoon dry mustard
½	Tablespoon Worcestershire
½	Tablespoon pepper
½	Tablespoon parsley flakes
1	pound crab meat
1	egg
1	cup Panko (Japanese breadcrumbs)

Directions

1. Whisk together mayonnaise, all spices and Worcestershire sauce and egg.
2. Fold Panko and crabmeat into mix.
3. Shape into 3-inch patties.
4. Sauté about 3 minutes on each side, until cooked through and serve.

Spicy Crab Dip

Makes 3 cups

Ingredients

1	pound fresh lump crab meat
1	teaspoon garlic, chopped
¼	cup jalapeño, chopped
¼	pound coarse shredded Monterey Jack cheese
1	teaspoon Worcestershire sauce
1	teaspoon hot sauce
½	teaspoon kosher salt
½	cup mayonnaise
½	cup fresh finely shredded Parmesan cheese

Directions

1. Preheat oven to 325° F.
2. Mix everything except crab meat and Parmesan cheese together.
3. Fold in crab meat until well incorporated.
4. Pour into 8 by 8-inch glass pan.
5. Top with Parmesan cheese.
6. Bake for 12 to 15 minutes or until it starts to bubble.
7. Serve in dish with crackers or flatbread crostini.

Chef's tip

The crab cake recipe works well with any mixture of seafood. It's a great way to use boiled shrimp, baked or grilled fish. Substitute 1 pound crab meat with 1 pound cooked fish or chopped shrimp.

Appetizers

Spicy Grilled Shrimp with Tamarind Orange Chutney

Makes approximately 6 to 8 servings

Ingredients for the Shrimp

¼	cup garam masala (see page 28)
3	Tablespoons coriander
2	Tablespoons turmeric
4	cloves garlic
1	2-inch piece of ginger, peeled and thinly sliced
1-2	teaspoons sriracha sauce
4	pounds large shrimp, peeled and deveined

Ingredients for the Chutney

16	ounces Florida orange juice
16	ounces tamarind purée
1	small red onion, thinly sliced
2	Tablespoons water, ice cold
1	Tablespoon cornstarch
2	Florida oranges, segmented
1	Tablespoon ground coriander
1	Tablespoon ground cumin
1	Tablespoon fresh ginger, grated
2	Tablespoons fresh cilantro, chopped

Directions for the Shrimp

1. Combine garam masala, coriander, turmeric, garlic, ginger and sriracha sauce in food processor.
2. Purée until smooth.
3. Rub mixture onto shrimp; marinate for 30 minutes.
4. Grill shrimp and serve with Tamarind Orange Chutney.

Directions for the Chutney

1. Heat orange juice, tamarind purée and red onion in a saucepan over medium heat; bring to a boil.
2. Lower heat; cook until reduced by about one-third.
3. In small bowl, whisk together water and cornstarch until dissolved; whisk in 1 cup hot orange juice mixture; pour cornstarch mixture into saucepan.
4. Add oranges, coriander, cumin, ginger and cilantro to saucepan; stir well and bring to a boil, stirring constantly.
5. When mixture reaches a boil, remove from heat and cool.

Sriracha sauce is a paste of chili peppers, vinegar, garlic, sugar and salt named after the seaside city of Si Racha, in the Chonburi Province of central Thailand, where it was first produced for dishes served at local seafood restaurants.

Recipe and photo courtesy of the Florida Citrus Commission.

Shrimp & Scallop Mousse

Makes 24 hors d'oeuvres

Ingredients

4	large scallops, chilled and well dried
1¼	teaspoons Old Bay seasoning
5	egg whites
12	grilled small shrimp, cleaned and halved

Use a 24 count mini muffin pan or two 12 count mini muffin pans

Directions

1. Preheat oven to 250° F.
2. Puree all ingredients except shrimp in food processor until light and fluffy.
3. Spray muffin tins lightly with oil.
4. Using a piping bag with no tip, squeeze ½ inch of mixture into mini muffin tins.
5. Bake at 250° F for 15 minutes or until set.
6. Remove from muffin tin, cool slightly, top with shrimp and serve on crackers.

Roasted Red Pepper Roll

Makes 10 rolls

Ingredients

2	roasted red peppers, cut into 5 equal strips
10	asparagus tips, 1 per roll, 1 inch longer than the pepper strips
3	Tablespoons extra-virgin olive oil
1	clove garlic, minced
5	salted capers, drained, rinsed and minced
1	sun-dried tomato in oil, minced
3	Tablespoons breadcrumbs
	Parsley, chopped
	Salt and pepper to taste

Directions

1. Preheat oven to 400° F.
2. Heat the oil in frying pan and sauté the garlic until golden.
3. Add capers, sun-dried tomatoes, and then the breadcrumbs.
4. Sauté over low heat, stirring often, then add the parsley, salt, and pepper.
5. Cover red pepper strips with equal portions of the breadcrumb mixture, then insert an asparagus tip.
6. Roll up red pepper slice and close with a toothpick.
7. Place on baking sheet.
8. Bake for 4 minutes.

Appetizers

Rosemary-Skewered Meatballs

Makes 4 skewers

Ingredients

½	pound lean ground lamb
¼	cup grated Greek Myzithra Cheese
1	large egg, fork beaten
2	teaspoons sun-dried tomato pesto
1	teaspoon grated lemon zest
1	teaspoon chopped fresh rosemary
4	sprigs of fresh rosemary, 6 inches long with leaves cleaned off at least two inches.

Directions

1. Preheat oven to 400° F.
2. Combine first 6 ingredients.
3. Roll into 12 balls and place on a baking sheet.
4. Bake for 12 minutes until the internal temperature reaches 160° F. Let stand until cool enough to handle.
5. Thread 3 meatballs onto each rosemary sprig, stripping away leaves from the stem to allow easy skewering.

Hot and Smokey Stuffed Dates

Makes 6 stuffed dates

Ingredients

6	fresh whole dates, pitted
1½	teaspoons real bacon bits
¾	teaspoon sambal chili sauce
6	pieces jalapeño Monterey Jack cheese, ¼ inch thick and 1½ inch long
6	roasted, salted smoked almonds

Directions

1. Preheat oven to 375° F.
2. Mix bacon, sambal and cheese.
3. Stuff each date with mixture.
4. Place on baking sheet.
5. Top each with one almond.
6. Bake for 10 minutes until cheese is melted.
7. Let stand until slightly cooled, then serve.

Pork Brochettes
Makes 24 skewers

Ingredients

2	pounds pork loin, cut into ¾ inch cubes
2	ounces white wine
2	ounces olive oil
2	large garlic cloves, crushed
½	teaspoon each paprika, chili powder, cayenne pepper
1	bay leaf
2	teaspoons fresh thyme
	salt and pepper to taste
24	bamboo skewers, soaked in water for 10 minutes

Directions

1. Arrange meat in a plastic or glass shallow dish.
2. Mix together all other ingredients.
3. Pour mixture over the meat, cover, and leave to marinate in the fridge for at least 8 hours, turning once or twice.
4. Thread three cubes onto each skewer and cook on a very hot grill, turning once until done or place on grill pan in preheated 350° F oven and bake for 6 to 10 minutes until done.

Appetizers

Shrimp and Bacon Brochettes

Makes 24 skewers

Ingredients

12	strips thinly sliced bacon, cut in half
24	medium to large uncooked shrimp, peeled and deveined
1	Tablespoon olive oil
	pepper to taste
2	lemons, quartered
24	skewers, soaked in water for 10 minutes

Directions

1. Preheat oven to 425° F.
2. Wrap each shrimp with a piece of bacon.
3. Secure the bacon to the shrimp with a skewer through the thickest part of the shrimp.
4. Drizzle with oil and season with pepper.
5. Roast in hot oven on a baking tray for 10 to 15 minutes.
6. Remove from oven and squeeze lemon wedges for juice over the skewers.
7. Serve immediately.

HUMUS BI TAHINA
Makes 2 cups humus

Ingredients

- 1 12 ounce can chick peas
- ½ teaspoon salt
- 1 clove garlic, crushed
- ½ cup oil
- 1 lemon, juiced
- 3 Tablespoons Tahini
- 2 Tablespoons parsley
- ¼ cup toasted pine nuts

Directions

1. Drain chick peas, reserving ½ cup liquid.
2. Mash peas through sieve into a bowl.
3. Add crushed garlic and remaining ingredients except parsley and pine nuts and mix well.
4. Place in serving bowl and garnish with parsley and pine nuts; serve as a spread with flat bread.

Chef's tip

To make Tahina, use mortar and pestle to mash sesame seeds into a paste.

Fast and easy humus: add all ingredients to blender and mix to a paste. Do not over blend.

GOAT CHEESE CROSTINIS
Makes 24 hors d'oeuvres

Ingredients

- 6 slices bread
- 2 Tablespoons olive oil
- ½ teaspoon lemon pepper
- ¾ cup crumbled goat cheese
- ½ cup grated Havarti cheese
- 1 Tablespoon butter
- 3 Tablespoon coarsely chopped capers
- 2 garlic cloves, thinly sliced
- 1/3 cup sun dried tomatoes in oil, blotted dry and finely chopped
- 2 Tablespoons fresh chives
- 2 Tablespoons fresh oregano

Directions

1. Preheat oven to 425° F.
2. Brush each side of bread with olive oil and cut into 4 triangles.
3. Bake 7 to 10 minutes until crisp.
4. Turn over. Sprinkle goat cheese and Havarti cheese over top.
5. Bake for another 7 minutes until cheese is melted and golden.
6. Arrange on a serving platter.
7. While bread is baking, melt butter in a frying pan on medium. Add capers and garlic and cook for about 5 minutes until garlic is golden.
8. Spoon over triangles and sprinkle with remaining 3 ingredients.

Appetizers

Vietnamese Spring Rolls
Makes 6 rolls

Ingredients

3	Tablespoons dried pork
16	sprigs cilantro
12	mint leaves
1	onion, cut in half and sliced in strips
2	Tablespoons Hoisin sauce
6	large shrimp, cooked and cut in half long ways
1	carrot, julienned into 2-inch strips
½	jicama, julienned into 2-inch strips
6	rice wraps

Directions

1. Sauté onion in 1 Tablespoon oil and 2 Tablespoons Hoisin sauce. Set aside in colander and let drain.
2. Dip each rice wrap in warm water and spread out on tray or cutting board.
3. Place shrimp halves outside down and tail to tail starting 3 inches from edge of wrap.
4. Top with a pinch of dried pork, then 3 or 4 strips of sautéed onions.
5. Arrange cilantro, mint leaves, carrots and jicama strips on top.
6. Fold bottom third of softened rice paper over top of shrimp and vegetables, then fold both sides over and roll up from bottom.
7. Serve with dipping sauce.

Vietnamese spring rolls, sometimes called summer rolls, may be served family style, allowing each person to roll their own. Arrange on plate and serve with spring roll dipping sauce on page 33.

Wild Rice Blini with Lemon Tarragon Cream

Makes 14 hors d'oeuvres

Ingredients

Blini

- ¼ cup cooked wild rice (see recipe on page 101)
- 1/3 cup pancake batter (see recipe on page 56)

Lemon Tarragon Cream

- 8 ounces cream cheese, softened
- Juice of one lemon
- 1 teaspoon fresh tarragon, minced

Thinly sliced smoked salmon for garnish

Directions

1. In a small bowl, mix together cream cheese, tarragon and lemon juice.
2. In a separate mixing bowl, combine cooked rice and pancake batter until just mixed.
3. Heat cooking oil in a small frying pan on medium.
4. Spoon 1 tablespoon batter in pan.
5. Cook until edges appear dry and bubbles form on top.
6. Turn mini-pancake. Cook until golden brown. Remove and repeat with remaining batter.
7. Garnish each mini-cake with lemon tarragon cream and smoked salmon.

Photo by John Sluder

Appetizers

Zucchini, Pear and Pecorino Cheese Tarts

Makes 12 tarts

Ingredients

½	pear diced into ¼ inch squares
1	Tablespoon extra virgin olive oil
1	garlic clove, crushed
3	zucchini, cut into matchsticks, no seeds
	Salt and pepper to taste
2	Tablespoons slivered almonds
5	ounces Pecorino cheese, shaved
1	sheet puff pastry, thawed and cut into 12 squares

Directions

1. Preheat oven to 375° F.
2. Brush puff pastry squares with olive oil.
3. Place Pecorino shavings onto each piece of puff pastry arranged on a baking sheet.
4. Bake for 10 minutes.
5. Meanwhile, In a frying pan, heat the olive oil and sauté the garlic until brown.
6. Remove and discard garlic, then add the zucchini and sauté over high heat for 3 minutes.
7. Add pear pieces and sauté for 2 more minutes
8. Season to taste with salt and pepper.
9. When pastry is done, top each puff pastry square with zucchini/pear sauce.
10. Serve hot.

Aussie Beef Pastries

Makes 8

Ingredients

1	teaspoon olive oil
½	pound diced tenderloin
½	cup red onion, diced
½	cup red pepper, diced
2	Tablespoons sun-dried tomato pesto
1	garlic clove, minced
¼	teaspoon salt
½	teaspoon pepper
½	sheet puff pastry, thawed

Directions

1. Preheat oven to 400° F.
2. Heat olive oil in a frying pan on medium.
3. Add next 8 ingredients and scramble fry until beef is no longer pink. Remove from heat.
4. Unroll pastry to a 12 x 12-inch square.
5. Cut into 8 triangles and transfer to a greased baking sheet.
6. Spoon 1 Tablespoon beef mixture into center of triangle, leaving a ¼ inch border; brush border with water.
7. Fold corner to corner and seal with a fork.
8. Bake for 10 to 15 minutes until pastry is golden.

VEGETARIAN PIES

Makes 18 small flat pies

Ingredients

2	large red peppers, chopped
2	medium onions, chopped
¼	cup walnuts
½	teaspoon lemon juice
	Salt and pepper to taste
18	small balls of dough; see basic dough recipe on page 47

Directions

1. Preheat oven to 450° F.
2. In food processor, combine red peppers, onions, walnuts and lemon juice and pulse until mixed well; set aside.
3. Flatten dough with tips of fingers.
4. Spoon 1 Tablespoon mixture onto each round of dough, but do not close.
5. Bake at 450° F for 10 to 15 minutes.

In memory of the Abody brothers, Joe (left) and John (right)

MEAT PIES

Makes 12 small appetizers

Ingredients

1	pound diced lamb
½	cup pine nuts
½	cup labanee (drawn yogurt)
1	onion, diced
	Juice of one lemon
	Salt and pepper to taste
12	small balls of dough; see basic dough recipe on page 47

Directions

1. Preheat oven to 450° F.
2. Mix lamb with onions, salt, pepper, and pine nuts.
3. Add labanee.
4. Roll out dough approximately 1/8 to ¼ inch thick.
5. Fill with meat mixture, wet edges and fold dough into a half circle, pressing edges with fork tines.
6. Place in buttered or oiled cookie sheet.
7. Bake at 450° F for about 15 minutes.

Labanee

Mix 2 pinches salt into ¾ cup plain yogurt; line a sieve with 2 layers cheesecloth and pour in yogurt. Set over bowl in refrigerator overnight for at least 12 hours.

The following ingredients may be substituted for Labanee:

1	green pepper, diced
1	ripe tomato, diced
6	sprigs fresh parsley, chopped
2	Tablespoons tahini (sesame seed paste)

Appetizers

Spinach Pies
Makes 24 appetizers

Ingredients

1	pound fresh spinach, washed and finely chopped
2	medium onions, diced
	Juice of one lemon
	Salt and pepper to taste
2	Tablespoons oil
1/8	cup pine nuts or chopped walnuts (optional)
½	cup Feta cheese (optional)
	Basic dough recipe (page 47)

Directions

1. Preheat oven to 400° F.
2. Sauté onions in oil until translucent. Add salt, pepper, lemon juice, nuts and spinach, tossing until wilted. Set aside to cool.
3. Roll out dough ¼ inch thick and cut into 4-inch circles with cookie cutter.
4. Place a small amount of cooled spinach mixture on one half of the circle.
5. Wet edges of dough with fingers dipped in water, fold dough over mixture to form a half moon, pressing sides closed with fork tines.
6. Place on greased cookie sheet and bake for 15 minutes or until golden brown.

Potato and Meat Pies
Makes 24 appetizers

Ingredients

2	pounds potatoes
1	pound coarsely ground lamb or beef, not too lean
1	Tablespoon butter
1	large onion, chopped
	Juice of 1 lemon
	Salt and pepper to taste
	Basic dough recipe (page 47)

Directions

1. Preheat oven to 400° F.
2. Grate potatoes and cover with cold water and 1 teaspoon salt; soak for 20 minutes or until needed.
3. Scoop potatoes by handfuls and squeeze out water before putting in a large bowl.
4. Combine potatoes with remaining ingredients except dough and mix well.
5. Roll out dough ¼ inch thick and cut into 4-inch circles with cookie cutter.
6. Place a small amount of the potato/meat mixture on one half of the circle.
7. Wet edges of dough with fingers dipped in water, fold dough over mixture to form a half moon; press sides closed with fork tines.
8. Place on greased cookie sheet and bake for 15 minutes until golden brown.

Photo courtesy of Wes Lineberry

ENTRÉES

Beef Short Ribs

Makes 6 servings

Ingredients

6	16-ounce beef short ribs
2	12-ounce beers, dark
3	celery sticks, chopped
1	medium onion, chopped
1	carrot, chopped
1	Tablespoon garlic, chopped
1	teaspoon cumin
2	Tablespoons tomato paste
1	tomato, chopped
1	Tablespoon oil

Directions

1. Arrange short ribs in bottom of large baking pan
2. Mix all other ingredients with beer and tomato sauce; blend well.
3. Pour over short ribs.
4. Bake at 325° F for 5 to 6 hours.
5. Serve hot.

Stuart's Shepherds Pie
Makes 8 servings

Ingredients

2	pounds ground beef
2	cups onion
1	teaspoon black pepper
½	teaspoon salt
2	cups carrots, diced
2	cups celery, chopped
1	cup corn
¼	cup Worcestershire sauce
1	cup soy sauce
½	cup A1 sauce
¾	cup catsup
1	teaspoon dry mustard
8	cups mashed potatoes
½	cup grated Cheddar cheese
½	teaspoon paprika for garnish

Directions

1. Preheat oven to 350° F.
2. Boil carrots and celery in small amount of water until tender.
3. Fry ground beef with onion, salt, pepper.
4. Add carrots, celery, corn, Worcestershire sauce, soy sauce, A1, catsup and dry mustard.
5. Place meat mix in bottom of round bowls for individual servings or a 9 X 12 baking pan for a family dinner.
6. Cover meat mixture with a layer of hot mashed potatoes. Garnish with Cheddar cheese and paprika.
7. Bake at 350° F for 20 to 25 minutes or until bubbling slightly around the edges.

To use leftover mashed potatoes, heat and add 2 ounces of hot butter then remix on high until smooth. Spread over meat mixture and bake as directed.

Entrees

Sesame Crusted Tuna
Makes 2 serving

Ingredients

16	ounces Cantonese noodles
6	baby corn
2	baby Bok Choy, cut lengthwise
2	8-ounce yellow fin tuna steaks
2	cups Ponzu sauce (see Stuart's recipe on page 32)
1	cup black and white sesame seeds
	Green sushi seaweed (optional)

Directions

1. Cook Cantonese noodles according to directions on package.
2. Drain and set aside.
3. Cover each tuna steak with black and white sesame seeds.
4. Sear tuna in a hot skillet, roughly 30 seconds on each side or until preferred temperature; remove and set aside.
5. Add vegetables to hot sauté pan, add Cantonese noodles and Ponzu sauce; cook until Bok Choy is wilted and corn and noodles are hot.
6. Divide evenly on two plates.
7. Top each with one tuna steak sliced in half and serve.

Photo by Karli Winkler

Chef's tip

Take four or five cooked noodles, wrapping the centers with a strip of seaweed, then deep fry. The desired effect is for the noodles to look like coral. Top with some micro greens and enjoy your gourmet sesame crusted tuna. Linguine is an easy substitute for Cantonese noodles. Instead of corn and Bok Choy, try using zucchini and yellow crookneck squash. This dish is also great using grouper instead of tuna.

Yellow Dog Café ™ Cookbook

Nancy's Gołumpki (Stuffed Cabbage)

Makes 4 servings

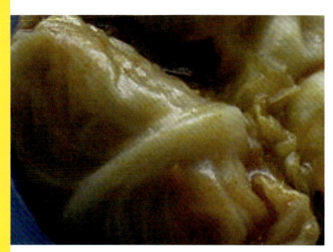

Ingredients

1	head cabbage (about 3 pounds)
½	pound ground pork
½	pound ground hamburger
2	cups cooked rice
1	small onion, chopped
1	stalk celery, chopped
1	small bell pepper, chopped
	dash salt and pepper
1	egg
1	8-ounce can tomato sauce

Directions

1. Preheat oven to 350° F.
2. Cut core out of whole cabbage and place in a cabbage size pot, fill with water half way up the cabbage.
3. Add 1 teaspoon salt.
4. Boil in covered pot until leaves start to blanche and are easy to separate from one another.
5. Using tongs and a fork, remove as many leaves as you can and set aside.
6. Cover remaining cabbage and repeat process until most leaves are removed.
7. In a large bowl, combine beef, pork, onion, celery, bell pepper, egg, rice, salt and pepper.
8. Mix well.
9. Once leaves are cool enough to touch, scoop a palm sized amount of meat mixture, forming a ball and place into one leaf.
10. Fold into a square and place fold side down in a covered baking dish or Dutch oven.
11. Repeat until all meat mixture is used up,
12. Pour tomato sauce over stuffed cabbages.
13. Bake in 350° F oven for 1½ hours or until meat is done.

Chef's tip

My editor's mom Gertruda Maxam was born in Poland, where her family replaced rice with cubed stale bread dipped in water then wrung out. Replace celery & bell pepper with basil and ½ cup ketchup. Arrange gołumpki (pronounced "go-wump´-key") in Dutch oven with small red potatoes; bake as instructed above. Note, this version leaves out tomato sauce. Any remaining cabbage may be cut into thin slices, then boiled for 2 minutes. Drain, cool and combine the leftover cabbage with one finely chopped onion. Toss with 2 Tablespoons vinegar, 2 Tablespoons oil, 1 teaspoon sugar, salt and pepper to taste for a great salad.

Entrees

Pork Chops with Tabasco Molasses Marinade
Makes 6 servings

Ingredients

7	Tablespoons molasses
7	Tablespoons Tabasco sauce
2	Tablespoons garlic, chopped
1	Tablespoon Worcestershire sauce
4	Tablespoons fresh thyme
1	cup salad oil
6	pork chops

Directions

1. Place molasses, Tabasco sauce, garlic, and Worcestershire sauce in blender.
2. Turn blender on medium and slowly add oil through cap until incorporated.
3. Stir thyme into marinade.
4. Set aside ½ cup marinade for sauce.
5. Place pork chops in glass dish, pour remaining marinade over top, then flip meat so all sides are covered.
6. Marinade overnight.
7. Grill meat to desired temperature and serve with reserved sauce.

Discard any marinade used to marinate pork chops.

Pork Medallions and Shrimp

Makes 1 serving

Ingredients

3	thin slices pork loin, pounded
3	shrimp, peeled and deveined
3	medium broccoli florets, blanched
3	large fresh mushrooms, sliced each in thirds
1	Tablespoon olive oil
2	Tablespoons butter
¼	teaspoon minced garlic
1	cup Ritz cracker crumbs with 1 Tablespoon parsley flakes
	egg wash (1 egg plus ¼ cup milk)
¼	cup white wine
	Hollandaise sauce (see Stuart's recipe on page 40)

Directions

1. In skillet or wok, heat olive oil on medium.
2. Dip pounded pork into egg wash then cracker crumbs.
3. Sauté pork on both sides to golden brown, remove from pan and keep warm.
4. In same pan, sauté the shrimp, broccoli, garlic and mushrooms in butter until shrimp is pink.
5. Deglaze with a splash of wine.
6. Arrange pork medallions in center of plate; top each with 1 shrimp, 1 broccoli floret and 3 slices of mushrooms and the pan drippings.
7. Garnish with 1 Tablespoon of Hollandaise sauce and serve.

Chef's tip

This recipe is for one but you can cook as many pork slices as the pan will hold at one time. Repeat process, adjusting other ingredients as necessary. Keep pork slices warm in oven until ready to serve.

MEATLOAF

Makes 4 servings

Ingredients

5	slices bread, cubed
2	eggs
½	cup onions chopped fine
½	cup celery, chopped fine
¼	cup oatmeal (scant)
¼	cup parmesan cheese, grated
½	Tablespoon garlic powder
¼	Tablespoon oregano, dried or fresh chopped
1	Tablespoon parsley, or to taste
1	teaspoon salt
½	teaspoon black pepper
1	pound ground beef

Directions

1. Preheat oven to 325° F.
2. Soak bread in water; place in colander and allow to drain.
3. Mix all ingredients, except meat and bread, in large mixing bowl.
4. Add beef and mix well.
5. Add wet bread and drag it through with your fingers, trying not to break up too much, but make sure it is well incorporated.
6. Shape into an oval and place in a 3 X 5 X 9 -inch loaf pan.
7. Bake for 45 minutes.

Serve with fresh vegetables, such as corn on the cob.

Broccoli with Beef

Makes 2 servings

Ingredients

½	pound sirloin steak
1	Tablespoon oil
½	cup broccoli florets
1	cup onions, thinly sliced
1	cup celery, thinly sliced
1	clove garlic, minced fine
¾	cup beef broth
1	Tablespoon sherry
½	teaspoon salt
¼	teaspoon pepper
1	Tablespoon cornstarch
3	Tablespoons water
2	cups cooked brown or white rice

Directions

1. Slice beef into thin strips.
2. In wok, heat oil and stir-fry the beef until browned.
3. Add broccoli, onions, celery, and garlic.
4. Stir-fry for 2 to 3 minutes.
5. Add beef broth, sherry, salt, and pepper.
6. Mix well, cover and cook 5 minutes or until broccoli is tender.
7. Stir cornstarch and water together into a thin paste.
8. Add to beef mixture.
9. Stir and cook until thickened.
10. Serve over hot rice.

Entrees

Shrimp and Pork with Bok Choy

Makes 2 servings

Ingredients

½	pound fresh shrimp, peeled, cleaned and deveined
1	Tablespoon oil
¼	pound ground pork
1	cup onions, thinly sliced
1	cup bean sprouts
2	cups Bok Choy, (Chinese white cabbage) thinly sliced
1	small green pepper, seeded and thinly sliced
¼	pound fresh mushrooms, thinly sliced
2	small tomato, diced fine
½	teaspoon salt
1/8	teaspoon pepper
½	cup chicken broth
1	Tablespoon cornstarch
3	Tablespoons water
1	Tablespoon soy sauce
2	cups cooked brown or white rice

Directions

1. In wok, heat oil and stir-fry shrimp.
2. When shrimp turns pink, remove with slotted spoon and set aside.
3. Sauté pork in wok until it crumbles.
4. Add vegetables and season with salt and pepper.
5. Stir-fry 2 to 3 minutes.
6. Add chicken broth.
7. Cover and cook 5 minutes longer.
8. Make a thin paste of the cornstarch, water, and soy sauce.
9. Sir into vegetables until thickened.
10. Return shrimp to wok and heat through.
11. Serve over hot rice.

Potato and Herb Gnocchi

Makes 8 servings

Ingredients

3¾	cups water
2¼	sticks butter plus extra for browning gnocchi kosher salt to taste
3	cups all purpose flour
3	eggs
1½	cups parmesan cheese, grated
3	cups mashed potatoes
1½	Tablespoons Dijon mustard
½	Tablespoon oregano, chopped
½	Tablespoon chives, chopped
½	Tablespoon parsley, chopped
½	Tablespoon tarragon, chopped

Directions

1. In stainless steel pot, combine water, butter and salt. Bring to boil; add flour; cook 5 to 8 minutes, stirring continuously, or until dough pulls away from bottom and leaves behind a thin layer of film.
2. Remove from pan and transfer to a stand mixer and mix dough on medium speed while adding eggs one at a time until incorporated.
3. Add parmesan, potatoes, mustard and herbs. Continue mixing until incorporated. (For a more robust dumpling, add an extra half cup flour.)
4. Place mixture in large pastry bag with no tip.
5. Pipe into long tubes (see photo above).
6. Slice into half inch lengths and let stand for at least 30 minutes in the refrigerator.
7. Bring a pot of salted water to a simmer. Line a baking sheet with paper towels. Line a second pan with parchment paper.
8. In small batches, drop gnocchi directly into simmering water.
9. Once the gnocchi floats to the top, simmer for about one minute, then remove them with a slotted spoon and drain on paper towel.
10. Once drained, place gnocchi in a single layer on the parchment paper-lined pan. Refrigerate for at least 30 minutes or up to a day before using. (May be frozen in a single layer for later use.)
11. In a large skillet, brown gnocchi in butter or olive oil until golden before serving. Top with your favorite sauce, such as Béchamel, marinara, mushroom Alfredo or saffron cream sauce (see page 32 for recipe).

Entrees

Shrimp Louisiana

Makes 2 servings

Ingredients

12	Tablespoons butter
1	teaspoon garlic, minced
1	pound shrimp, peeled, deveined, tail on
1	teaspoon Worcestershire sauce
1½	Tablespoons Shrimp Louisiana seasoning mix (see recipe at right)
¼	cup dark beer (preferably Abita Turbo Dog)
½	cup shrimp stock

Directions

1. In sauté pan on medium heat, combine 8 Tablespoons butter, garlic, Worcestershire sauce and seasoning mix.
2. Add shrimp, cook three minutes; and flip shrimp.
3. Add remaining 4 Tablespoons butter and shrimp stock; cook for an additional three minutes without stirring.
4. Add ¼ cup beer to deglaze pan.
5. Reduce until creamy and serve with grits or rice.

Shrimp Louisiana Seasoning Mix

Makes 2 Tablespoons

Ingredients

1	teaspoon cayenne pepper
1	teaspoon black pepper
½	teaspoon salt
½	teaspoon red pepper flakes
½	teaspoon thyme
½	teaspoon rosemary
½	teaspoon Old Bay seasoning (optional)
	Pinch oregano

Directions

Combine all ingredients and use as directed.

Yellow Dog Café ™ Cookbook

Chicken Piccata

Makes 2 servings

Ingredients

- 2 boneless chicken breasts (pounded)
- ½ cup flour seasoned with salt and pepper
- 1 Tablespoon capers
- 1 teaspoon garlic
- 1 teaspoon fresh parsley, chopped
- 1 ounce lemon juice
- 1 ounce white wine
- 2 Tablespoons stick butter, softened

Chef's tip

Place chicken breasts inside gallon size freezer bag before pounding to cut down on splatter.

Directions

1. Dredge chicken in seasoned flour.
2. Sauté in olive oil until browned and cooked thoroughly, about 7 minutes, turning once.
3. Remove from pan.
4. Add capers, garlic, lemon juice, white wine to pan and reduce by half.
5. Return chicken to pan with butter and parsley.
6. Cook, shaking pan until butter is melted.
7. Serve sauce over chicken.

Stuffed Pork Chops

Makes 6 servings

Ingredients

6	1½ - inch thick boneless pork chops
1	cup cooked rice
2	Tablespoons chopped green pepper
2	Tablespoons chopped onion
½	teaspoon each paprika, celery seed, black pepper, garlic powder and salt
2	Tablespoons grated Parmesan cheese
2	Tablespoons shortening
1	cup red onion marmalade (see recipe on page 39)
¼	cup water

Directions

1. Preheat oven 350° F.
2. Cut a pocket in each chop using a sharp paring knife; slicing horizontally from the non-fat side of the meat about ¾ of the way through, leaving a seam on three sides.
3. Mix rice, green pepper, onion, salt, and spices in a 2-quart bowl.
4. Stuff rice mixture inside each pork pocket.
5. In hot sauté pan, brown chops in shortening, about 1 minute each side.
6. Place stuffed chops in shallow 2-quart baking dish.
7. Mix marmalade and water together and pour over chops.
8. Cover with foil and bake for 45 minutes or until pork is tender.

Onion Crusted Chicken with Caramel Citrus Glaze

Makes 2 servings

Ingredients

2	8-ounce boneless chicken breasts
½	pound bacon, chopped fine
½	red onion, chopped fine
1	cup sugar
1	Tablespoon tomato puree
2	cups water
1	orange, juiced
1	lemon, juiced
1	lime, juiced
¼	cup vegetable oil
	Salt and pepper to taste
1	egg, beaten
¼	cup milk for dredging
1	cup fried onions, chopped (see page 105 for recipe)

Directions

1. In a non-stick skillet, cook bacon and onions until onion is translucent.
2. Add sugar, water and tomato puree and reduce mixture until thick.
3. Add citrus juices and stir well. Set aside glaze.
4. In a non-stick skillet, heat oil on medium setting.
5. Season chicken with salt and pepper.
6. Dip chicken into beaten egg and milk, then press into fried onions.
7. Place chicken in heated skillet and cook for 10 minutes, turning once until golden and cooked through.
8. Place on serving plate and spoon glaze over chicken.
9. Serve with rice or mashed potatoes accompanied by fresh vegetables.

Entrees

Potato Crusted Salmon
Serves 4

Ingredients

4	salmon filets
1	potato, sliced into 1/8-inch circles
4	Tablespoons butter, melted
	Salt and pepper to taste
	Oil for sautéing

Directions

1. Melt butter and brush salmon on skinless side.
2. Cover the skinless side with slices of potato.
3. Sauté in about ¼-inch oil, potato side down, about 5 minutes.
4. Turn and cook until salmon is done.
5. Serve potato side up topped with saffron cream sauce (see recipe on page 32).

This recipe is also pictured on the front cover.

154

DESSERTS

155

S'mores Cheesecake

This is a combination of three recipes.

Makes 12 servings

Ingredients

Half the cheesecake recipe (see page 159)

Half the brownies recipe (see page 158)

One batch marshmallows (see page 157)

Directions

1. Preheat oven to 225° F.
2. Make crust according to recipe on page 159, pressing crackers into bottom of a 9-inch round spring-form pan.
3. Prepare half the cheesecake filling on page 159; pour on top of crust in spring-form pan and bake at 225° F for 40 minutes.
4. Let cool and chill in refrigerator for at least 6 hours.
5. Preheat oven to 325° F.
6. Prepare half the brownie recipe on page 158.
7. Pour uncooked brownie mixture on top of chilled cheesecake.
8. Bake brownie/cheesecake for 8 minutes.
9. While brownies are baking, make marshmallow recipe, using steps 1 through 3 on page 157.
10. When brownies are done, pour marshmallow topping over warm brownie, spreading with the back of a wet spoon.
11. Brown with a torch or under the broiler until marshmallow turns golden brown.
12. Serve while brownie is still warm.

Yellow Dog Café ™ Cookbook

Yellow Dog Marshmallows

Makes 36 1¼ X 1¾ - inch pieces

Ingredients

4	teaspoons gelatin
½	cup hot water
1¼	cups granulated sugar
¼	cup cold water
1	teaspoon flavoring (your choice of vanilla, mint, strawberry, rum, etc.)
1	cup confectioners sugar, sifted and set aside for covering finished marshmallows

Directions

1. Combine gelatin and hot water, stir and let stand until dissolved.
2. Once dissolved, in a mixer bowl add granulated sugar and cold water.
3. Whip on high speed for 5 minutes or until light and fluffy.
4. Spread mixture in an 8 X 11 pan lined with parchment paper lightly dusted with confectioners sugar.
5. Let dry for at least 2 hours before cutting into squares with knife or scissors dusted with confectioners sugar.
6. Store marshmallows layered with remaining confectioners sugar in an airtight container.

Desserts

Stuart's House Brownies
Makes 12 servings

Ingredients

- 1 cup margarine or butter
- 2 cups sugar
- 2 teaspoons vanilla
- 4 eggs
- ¾ cup cocoa
- 1 cup flour
- ½ teaspoon baking powder
- ¼ teaspoon salt
- 1 cup chopped walnuts

Directions

1. Preheat oven to 350° F.
2. Melt butter.
3. Stir in sugar and vanilla.
4. Add eggs one at a time, beating after each egg.
5. Add cocoa.
6. Beat until well blended.
7. Add flour, baking powder and salt. Beat well.
8. Stir in nuts and pour into greased 9 X 13 X 2 inch pan.
9. Bake for 18 minutes.
10. Let cool and top with chocolate ganache (recipe on page 166).

Cheesecake

Makes 1 nine-inch cheesecake; serves 8

Ingredients

Crust

2	dozen graham crackers
2/3	cup brown sugar
½	cup melted butter or margarine

Filling

2	pounds cream cheese, softened
1¼	cups sugar
¼	cup cornstarch
4	eggs
1	teaspoon vanilla
1	Tablespoon lemon juice

Directions

Crust

1. Place graham crackers into a plastic bag and roll with rolling pin until finely crushed.
2. Stir in butter and brown sugar until well blended. Press into bottom of 9-inch spring form pan.

Filling

3. Preheat oven to 225° F.
4. Mix softened cream cheese on low speed for one minute.
5. Combine sugar and cornstarch together and add to cream cheese.
6. Mix until combined.
7. Scrap sides of bowl.
8. Add eggs and lemon juice
9. Mix until thoroughly combined, scraping down sides occasionally.
10. Pour into prepared crust.
11. Bake at 225° F for 1 hour or until set.
12. Cool in pan for 6 hours or overnight.
13. Top with favorite fruit or serve plain with raspberry sauce (see recipe on page 38).

Desserts

Apple Cinnamon Crepes

Makes 2 servings

Ingredients

4-6	prepared crepes (see recipe on page 55)
16	ounces cream cheese, softened
1	cup apple pie filling
1	Tablespoon cinnamon
1	Tablespoon sugar
1	Tablespoon caramel topping

Directions

1. Whip cream cheese until light and fluffy. Fold in pie filling, cinnamon and sugar.
2. Heat over double boiler or in microwave until warm.
3. Add approximately 2 to 3 tablespoons of filling onto crepe and spread evenly.
4. Fold crepe in half and then half again. Place desired number of crepes on plate and top with caramel.
5. You may substitute the apple pie filling with strawberry, blueberry or cherry pie filling, omitting the cinnamon and caramel topping.

Chef's tip

Save leftover crepes, layered between wax paper. Fill with chicken or tuna salad and microwave for 30 seconds. For a quick appetizer, place one large Tablespoon of crab dip on crepe and fold crepe in quarters and top with Hollandaise sauce.

Crème Brûlée

Makes 12 servings

Ingredients

1	quart heavy cream
5	large eggs
1	vanilla bean or 1 teaspoon vanilla extract
¾	cup sugar
2	teaspoons cornstarch
12	Tablespoons sugar for caramelizing

Chef's tip: The vanilla bean should be split long ways and scraped using the side of a knife to gather the seeds. The outer shell may be used to flavor sugar by placing it in an airtight container covered with granulated sugar. The resulting vanilla flavored sugar is excellent to caramelize on the top of the Crème Brûlée.

Directions

1. Combine all ingredients and mix in blender until smooth.
2. Pour into heavy bottomed pan and cook on medium to high heat, stirring constantly.
3. After the mixture starts its first bubble, stir for one minute and remove from heat.
4. Strain through a sieve to remove pieces of vanilla bean.
5. Pour into 12 ramekins. Cool, then wrap and refrigerate.
6. Before serving, sprinkle each top with 1 Tablespoon sugar and caramelize with a torch until the topping becomes brittle.
7. Serve immediately.

Desserts

Stuart's Bread Pudding

Makes 10 ramekins or one 9 X 12-inch baking dish

Ingredients

8 -10 slices bread cut into 1 inch chunks, dried
Crème Brûlée ingredients (see previous page) **without** the cornstarch

Directions

1. Allow bread chunks to dry.
2. Fill 8 ramekins or a baking dish ½ full with bread chunks and set aside.
3. Preheat oven to 350° F.
4. Mix cream, eggs, vanilla and sugar in blender until smooth.
5. Pour into ramekins or a baking dish, poking the bread into the liquid until all pieces are coated.
6. Sprinkle cinnamon on top and place ramekins or baking dish in a water bath inside the oven.
7. Cover water bath and bread pudding with foil and bake for 45 minutes or until the pudding is cooked all the way through with a spring to the touch.
8. Serve warm and topped with Yellow Dog whisky sauce featured on this page.

Yellow Dog Whiskey Sauce

Ingredients

1	cup heavy cream
2/3	cup sugar
3	egg yolks
1	Tablespoon whiskey

Directions

1. Combine all ingredients except whiskey in a sauce pan.
2. Cook on low heat, whisking continuously until mixture boils.
3. Remove from heat and stir in whiskey.
4. Serve immediately.

Chef's tip

For a water bath, place your pudding dish into a deep roasting pan, place the pan into the oven, and then add enough hot water to reach halfway up the pan.

Photo by John Sluder

Basic Muffins

Makes 3 dozen regular muffins

Ingredients

1	stick butter, softened
1	cup sugar
1	cup boiling water
2½	teaspoons baking soda
2½	cups sugar
2	eggs
2	cups buttermilk (or regular milk mixed with 2 Tablespoons white vinegar)
4½	cups flour
1	cup oats

Directions

1. Preheat oven to 350° F.
2. Cream butter and sugar.
3. Add boiling water and baking soda.
4. Stir and let cool for a few minutes.
5. In a separate bowl, mix sugar, eggs, buttermilk, flour and oats.
6. Combine all ingredients together, folding until well incorporated.
7. Fill muffin cups ¾ full.
8. Bake at 350° F for 20 minutes or until lightly browned.

Chef's tip

This recipe is quite versatile. Try sprinkling a crumb topping mix on top (see recipe on page 167) or folding 1 cup M & M's, fresh blueberries, chocolate chips, cranberries or even grated carrots into the batter before baking. Batter may also be kept in refrigerator for 3 to 4 days, covered, so you can make a few fresh muffins every day.

Mississippi Mud Cake

Makes 8 to 10 servings

Ingredients

2	cups flour
1	teaspoon baking soda
1¾	cups strong coffee
½	cup bourbon
5	ounces bitter chocolate, cut up
1	cup butter
2	cups sugar
2	eggs lightly beaten
1	teaspoon vanilla
1	9-inch Bundt pan dusted with cocoa powder

Directions

1. Preheat oven to 275° F.
2. Sift together flour and baking soda.
3. Heat coffee and bourbon on top of double boiler until warm.
4. Add chocolate and butter, stirring until melted and smooth. Remove from heat.
5. Stir in sugar and cool for 3 minutes.
6. Transfer to mixing bowl.
7. Add flour to chocolate mixture ½ cup at a time and mix on low speed.
8. Continue to beat for 1 minute.
9. Add eggs and vanilla, beating until smooth.
10. Butter a 9-inch Bundt pan and dust with cocoa powder.
11. Pour mix in Bundt pan; bake for 1 hour and 15 minutes.
12. Cool completely in pan; flip onto serving tray; serve with soft whipped cream.

Mommy's Chocolate Cake

Makes 12 servings

Ingredients

1½	cups sifted flour
1¼	cups sugar
½	cup cocoa powder
1¼	teaspoon soda
¼	teaspoon cream of tartar
1	teaspoon salt
½	cup shortening
1	cup milk
1	Tablespoon vanilla
2	unbeaten eggs
2	teaspoons olive oil

Directions

1. Preheat oven to 350°F.
2. Mix all ingredients together in the above order into mixing bowl.
3. Beat on medium until well blended.
4. Pour batter into greased and floured 9 X 12-inch pan.
5. Bake for 25 to 30 minutes or until toothpick test indicates the batter is fully cooked.
6. Frost with icing of your choice or ganache (see recipe on page 166).

Desserts

Butter Icing

Makes enough to ice one 8-10 inch cake

Ingredients

1	pound powdered sugar
1	stick butter
1	Tablespoon vanilla
¼	cup milk

Directions

1. Sift powdered sugar.
2. Whip butter until it turns white.
3. Slowly add milk and vanilla.
4. Add powdered sugar and continue whipping until light and fluffy.

Creamy Icing

Makes enough to ice one 8-10 inch cake

Ingredients

1	cup milk
4	Tablespoons flour
2/3	cup shortening
1	teaspoon vanilla
2	cups powdered sugar

Directions

1. Cook milk and flour over low heat until thick.
2. Cool.
3. Add shortening, vanilla and powdered sugar.
4. Whip with mixer until it resembles whipped cream.

Chocolate Ganache

Makes 3 cups

Ingredients

2	cups chocolate chips
1	cup butter

Directions

1. In microwave safe container, heat butter until it bubbles, add chips and stir until smooth. If chips don't melt completely, return to microwave in 10 second intervals, stirring after each heating until completely smooth.
2. Use for icing cakes when mixture is still warm by pouring over top, allowing it to drizzle down sides.
3. May also shape mixture into melon-ball size rounds once cooled, then roll in cocoa or chopped nuts for a homemade truffle.

Graham Cracker Pie Crust

Makes 1 nine-inch pie crust

Ingredients

2	dozen graham crackers
2/3	cup brown sugar
½	cup melted butter or margarine

Directions

1. Preheated oven to 350°F.
2. Place crackers in a plastic bag and roll with rolling pin until finely crushed.
3. Measure 2 cups graham cracker crumbs into a medium bowl with brown sugar.
4. Stir in melted butter until blended.
5. Press into pie plate.
6. Bake 8 to 10 minutes.
7. If used for cheesecake, omit baking and simply press into bottom and side of pan, fill with batter and then bake according to cake recipe.

Crumb Topping

Makes enough for 1 batch of muffins or 1 pie

Ingredients

1/3	cup flour
¼	cup brown sugar
¼	teaspoon cinnamon
2	Tablespoons butter, softened

Directions

1. Toss flour, brown sugar and cinnamon in bowl.
2. Cut butter into dry mixture with a pastry blender until it resembles course crumbs.
3. Sprinkle on top of muffins or apple pie and bake according to muffin/pie directions.

Desserts

NEVER FAIL PIE CRUST
Makes 1 nine to 10-inch pie crust, top and bottom

Ingredients

3	cups flour
1	cup shortening
1	Tablespoon salt
1	egg
2	Tablespoons vinegar
	Ice water

Directions

1. Mix flour, shortening, salt, blending with a pastry cutter.
2. Add egg and vinegar and blend in.
3. Add just enough water, teaspoon by teaspoon, to make a soft dough.
4. Divide dough in half.
5. Roll dough into two circles on floured surface.
6. Use as instructed in pie recipes.

Chef's tip
Left over dough may be rolled out, egg washed and sprinkled with cinnamon and sugar. Place on a cookie sheet, slice into strips and bake at 350°F for 15 minutes or until done. Enjoy this easy snack while you wait for your pie.

BUTTER CRUST FOR PIES
Makes 1 nine to ten-inch crust, top and bottom

Ingredients

3	cups flour
¾	cup butter
1¼	cups shortening
1	teaspoon salt
1	cup water

Directions

1. In mixer, combine flour, butter, shortening and salt.
2. Mix on low until consistency of meal.
3. Add water a little at a time and mix on low, being careful not to over mix until it just comes together. You may not need all the water.
4. Divide dough in half.
5. Roll dough into two circles on floured surface.
6. Use as instructed in pie recipes.

Peanut Butter Custard Pie

Makes 8 servings

Ingredients

1	cup powdered sugar
¼	teaspoon vanilla
2/3	cup granulated sugar
3	egg yolks
½	cup creamy peanut butter
¼	cup corn starch
2	cups milk

9 ounces whipped topping
1 9-inch deep dish pie pan with pre-baked crust (see recipe on page 168)
Or graham cracker pie crust on page 167

Directions for pre-baking pie crust

Prick bottom of dough with fork tines, cover with parchment paper and fill the inside with just enough dried beans or rice to hold the pie dough against the side of the pan; bake at 425°F for 20 minutes, remove parchment and weights and cool before use.

Directions

1. Mix powdered sugar and peanut butter in a bowl until crumbly using a hand mixer.
2. In a sauce pan, heat milk, egg yolks, corn starch, sugar and vanilla until custard thickens.
3. Spread one third of the peanut butter mixture in bottom of the pre-baked pie shell.
4. Pour half of custard in the pie shell.
5. Use the second third of peanut butter mixture to layer over the custard, reserving the remaining third for later.
6. Pour in remaining custard.
7. Cool pie in refrigerator.
8. Before serving, add Cool Whip and sprinkle with remaining peanut butter mixture.

Desserts

Peanut Butter Pie
Makes 8 servings

Ingredients

8	ounces cream cheese, softened
8	ounces whipped topping
¾	cup peanut butter
1½	cups powdered sugar
1	Graham cracker crust (page 167)

Directions

1. Whip cheese and powdered sugar until light and fluffy.
2. Whip in peanut butter.
3. When smooth, fold in whipped topping and pour into crust.
4. Sprinkle grated chocolate over top if desired.
5. Chill before serving.

Peanut Butter Oatmeal Cookies
Makes 7 dozen

Ingredients

3	cups quick cooking oats
1½	cups flour
½	teaspoon baking soda
¾	cup butter flavored shortening
1	cup peanut butter
1½	cups firmly packed brown sugar
½	cup water
1	egg
1	teaspoon vanilla

Directions

1. Preheat oven to 350° F.
2. In separate bowl, combine oats, flour and baking soda. Set aside.
3. In a mixer bowl, beat shortening, butter and brown sugar until creamy.
4. Beat in water, egg and vanilla.
5. Add combined dry ingredients.
6. Mix well.
7. Cover and chill in refrigerator about 2 hours.
8. Shape dough into one inch balls.
9. Place on ungreased cookie sheet.
10. Flatten with tines of a fork dipped in granulated sugar to form crisscross pattern.
11. Bake 9 to 11 minutes or until edges are golden brown.
12. Cool one minute on cookie sheet.
13. Remove to wire rack.
14. Cool completely before storing in tightly covered container.

Nancy's Amazing Coconut Pie

Makes 8 servings

Ingredients

- 2 cups milk
- ¾ cup sugar
- ½ cup Bisquick mix
- 4 eggs
- ¼ cup butter
- 1½ teaspoon vanilla
- 1 cup coconut for topping

Directions

1. Preheat oven to 350° F.
2. Combine milk, sugar, Bisquick mix, eggs, butter and vanilla.
3. Blend with mixer on low speed for three minutes
4. Pour into a greased pie dish.
5. Let stand for 5 minutes.
6. Sprinkle coconut over top.
7. Bake in center of oven at 350° F for 40 minutes.
8. Chill and serve.

To: Yellow Dog Cafe
Love, Niko

Desserts

Real Pumpkin Pie

Makes 8 servings

Crust Ingredients

1	cup flour
½	teaspoon salt
¼	Tablespoon sugar
½	cup shortening
1	egg
1½	Tablespoons water (ice cold)
¼	Tablespoon vinegar

*Contributed by **Jill Jones**, Winner 2009 National Pie Counsel Competition, Amateur division. Jill lives in Palm Bay, Florida just around the corner from the restaurant. We're very proud to feature her winning recipe!*

Crust Directions

1. Mix flour, salt, sugar, then cut in shortening with fork or pastry cutter until crumbly.
2. Add egg, water and vinegar.
3. Scrape out of bowl onto floured surface.
4. Roll into ball, plastic wrap and refrigerate ½ to 1 hour. Roll dough onto a floured surface.
5. Transfer into a pie pan.

Filling Ingredients

1	4 to 6-inch cooking pumpkin
¾	cup sugar
½	teaspoon salt
1	teaspoon cinnamon
¾	teaspoon pumpkin pie spice
1	smidgen fresh ground nutmeg
¼	teaspoon pure vanilla
2	eggs
1	14-ounce can sweetened condensed milk

Filling Directions

6. Cut pumpkin in half, scrape out seeds and string membranes of pumpkin.
7. Quarter pumpkin and in a double steamer, steam pumpkin until soft and skin peels off by touch (45 minutes to 1 hour).
8. Mash with potato masher then squeeze water out of mashed pumpkin through cheese cloth.
9. Mix pumpkin, sugar, salt, cinnamon, pumpkin pie spice, nutmeg, vanilla and mix well.
10. Add eggs and milk. Mix well.
11. Pour into unbaked pie crust.
12. Bake 425° F for 15 minutes.
13. Reduce heat to 350° F and cover crust edge.
14. Bake for 40 to 50 minutes.
15. Let cool 3 hours before serving.
16. Refrigerate.

Key Lime Pie

Makes 8 servings

Ingredients

1	can sweetened condensed milk
4	eggs, separated (reserve whites)
½	cup key lime juice
1	9-inch prepared Graham cracker pie crust (see recipe on page 167)

Directions

1. Preheat oven to 350° F.
2. In mixing bowl, beat milk for two minutes on high.
3. Add yolks and mix for 1 minute on high.
4. Add key lime juice and mix on high for another minute and set aside.
5. Beat one egg white to stiff peaks.
6. Fold egg white into key lime mixture.
7. Pour mixture into prepared Graham cracker pie crust.
8. Bake 12 to 15 minutes.
9. Cool to room temperature, chill before serving and garnish with whipped cream.

Coconut Cream Pie

Makes 8 servings

Ingredients

- ¾ cup sugar
- ¼ cup cornstarch
- 1/8 Tablespoon salt
- 3 cups milk
- 4 egg yolks, beaten
- ¾ cup flaked coconut
- 1½ Tablespoons butter
- 1 teaspoon vanilla

- 1 9-inch pie shell, pre-baked (see page 168 for recipe; and page 169 for pre-baking instructions)

Directions

1. Combine first three ingredients in a heavy sauce pan.
2. Combine milk and egg yolks, gradually stirring in sugar mixture.
3. Cook over medium heat, stirring constantly until mixture thickens and boils.
4. Boil one minute, stirring constantly.
5. Remove from heat and stir in ½ cup of the coconut, the butter and vanilla.
6. Pour immediately into baked pastry shell.
7. After pie cools, spread fresh whipped cream over top.
8. Sprinkle with remaining ¼ cup coconut flakes and serve.

Pictured as a personal pie as served at Yellow Dog Café in individual ramekins.

Butterscotch Pie

Makes 8 servings

Ingredients

¾	cup brown sugar
¼	cup white sugar
1/3	cup cornstarch
2	cups scalding milk
1/8	teaspoon salt
3	egg yolks
1½	Tablespoons butter
1	teaspoon vanilla
1	9-inch pre-baked pie shell (see pages 168 & 169)

Directions

1. In saucepan combine egg yolks, sugars, cornstarch and salt.
2. Add milk and cook over medium heat until it bubbles for 30 seconds, stirring constantly.
3. Remove from heat; whisk in butter and vanilla.
4. Pour into pie shell.
5. Cool, top with whipped cream and serve.

Pecan Pie

Makes 8 servings

Ingredients

3	eggs, beaten
1	cup sugar, brown or white
1	cup light corn syrup
1	cup pecan halves
1	teaspoon vanilla
½	stick melted butter
1	9-inch unbaked pie crust (see pages 168 & 169)

Directions

1. Preheat oven to 350° F.
2. Beat eggs, sugar, salt and corn syrup until blended.
3. Add pecans, butter and vanilla and mix well.
4. Pour into pie shell and bake at for one hour.

Desserts

Lemon Meringue Pie

Makes 8 servings

Ingredients

1	cup sugar
3	Tablespoons flour
4	Tablespoons cornstarch
1/8	teaspoon salt
1½	cups boiling water
	zest of 1 lemon
	juice of 2 lemons
3	egg yolks
½	Tablespoon butter
1	9-inch pastry shell, pre-baked (see pages 168 & 169)

Meringue

4	egg whites
¼	cup plus 2 Tablespoons sugar
¼	teaspoon cream of tartar

Directions

1. Fill bottom of double boiler with two inches of water and bring to a simmer.
2. In top of double boiler, mix sugar, flour, cornstarch and salt.
3. Add 1½ cups boiling water into sugar mixture slowly; stir until smooth.
4. Remove from double boiler, place on top of stove and cook, stirring constantly until it starts to boil.
5. Place back on double boiler and cook 20 minutes over hot water, stirring constantly.
6. Mix lemon zest, juice and egg yolks, slightly beaten, and add to mixture in double boiler.
7. Add butter and stir/cook for 2 minutes.
8. Cool and pour into the pre-baked crust.

Meringue

9. Preheat oven to 350° F.
10. Beat room temperature egg whites and cream of tartar at high speed for one minute.
11. Gradually add remaining sugar one tablespoon at a time.
12. Beat until stiff peaks form and sugar dissolves, 2 to 4 minutes.
13. Spread meringue over hot filling, sealing to edge of pastry.
14. Bake at 350° F for 8 minutes.
15. Cool and serve.

Banana Cream Pie

Makes 8 servings

Ingredients

¾	cup sugar
¼	cup cornstarch
1/8	teaspoon salt
3	cups milk
4	egg yolks, beaten
1½	Tablespoons butter or margarine
1	teaspoon vanilla
2	bananas
1	9-inch Graham cracker crust (see recipe on page 167)

Directions

1. Combine first three ingredients in a heavy sauce pan.
2. Combine milk and egg yolks and gradually stir into sugar mixture.
3. Cook over medium heat, stirring constantly until mixture thickens and boils.
4. Boil one minute, stirring constantly.
5. Remove from heat, stir in butter and vanilla.
6. Slice bananas into crust.
7. Pour hot filling over bananas.
8. Cover with plastic wrap and chill.
9. Before serving, remove plastic wrap, top with whipped cream.

Photo by John Sluder

Desserts

Chocolate Cream Pie

Makes 8 servings

Ingredients

1	cup sugar
¼	cup cocoa
¼	cup plus 1 Tablespoon cornstarch
1	Pinch salt
3	cups milk
4	egg yolks
1¼	Tablespoons vanilla
1	9-inch pre-baked graham cracker crust (see recipe on page 167)

Directions

1. Combine first 4 ingredients in a heavy sauce pan.
2. In separate bowl, combine milk and egg yolks.
3. Gradually stir into sugar mixture and cook over medium heat, stirring constantly until mixture thickens and boils.
4. Boil one minute, stirring constantly, then remove from heat and stir in vanilla. Immediately pour into pie crust.
5. Cover with plastic wrap and chill.
6. When ready to serve, remove plastic and top pie with fresh whipped cream.

New Zealand Kiwi Cheese Cake

Makes 8 servings

Ingredients

Ginger snap crust

1   cup crushed ginger snap cookies or Graham crackers (crushed)
½   stick butter, melted
1   nine-inch spring form cake pan

Filling

4   large kiwi fruit
1   pound (16 ounces) ricotta cheese
1   Tablespoon gelatin
1   cup heavy whipping cream, lightly whipped
1   teaspoon lemon juice
½   cup castor sugar (see tip below)
4   Tablespoons water
Kiwi fruit slices for garnish

Directions

1. Thoroughly mix crushed cookies or Graham crackers with melted butter.
2. Press crumbs into the base of a lightly greased 9-inch spring form cake pan.
3. Chill until required.
4. Peel kiwi fruit, cut into quarters, cut out seeds and discard.
5. Puree fruit in a blender or rub through a sieve.
6. Stir lemon juice into pureed fruit.
7. Place ricotta cheese in a large mixing bowl and beat in sugar until smooth.
8. Stir in kiwi fruit puree.
9. In a separate small bowl, sprinkle gelatin over water.
10. Stir to dissolve over hot water, allow to cool slightly.
11. Stir gelatin into ricotta cheese mixture then fold in whipped cream.
12. Pour into prepared spring form cake pan. Chill in refrigerator several hours to set.
13. Remove rim from pan and place cheese cake on a flat serving dish.
14. Decorate top with slices of kiwi fruit.

Chef's tip

To make castor sugar, blend regular sugar in a blender until very fine.

Desserts

Apple Crumb Pie

Makes 8 servings

Ingredients

1	nine-inch pre-made pie crust, unbaked bottom only (see recipe on page 168)
6	cups peeled, sliced cooking apples
½	cup granulated sugar
1	teaspoon ground cinnamon
½	teaspoon ground nutmeg
¼	cup flour
	Dash ground cloves (optional)
	Crumb topping (see recipe on page 167)

Directions

1. Preheat oven to 375° F.
2. In separate bowl, toss sliced apples with sugar, flour, cinnamon, nutmeg and cloves.
3. Pack apple mixture into the pie shell
4. Top with crumb topping.
5. Bake for 50 minutes or until apples are soft and crumb topping is brown.

Nancy's Orange Crisps

Makes 3 dozen

Ingredients

2	cups flour
¼	teaspoon baking soda
½	teaspoon salt
1	cup butter, softened
1	cup white sugar
½	cup brown sugar
1	teaspoon orange peel
2	eggs
2	cups raisin bran

Directions

1. Preheat oven to 350° F.
2. Mix flour, baking soda, and salt and set aside.
3. In mixer bowl, beat butter, white and brown sugar, and orange peel until smooth.
4. Add eggs and beat well.
5. Add dry ingredients and raisin bran and mix until combined.
6. Drop by level Tablespoons on ungreased baking sheet
7. Bake at 350° F for 15 minutes.

Custard Chiffon Cake

Makes 12 servings

Ingredients

¾	cup scalding hot milk
7	egg yolks, slightly beaten (reserve whites)
2	cups sifted flour
1½	cups sugar
1	teaspoon salt
1	Tablespoon baking powder
½	cup canola oil
2	teaspoons vanilla
1	cup egg whites
½	teaspoon cream of tartar
1	nine-inch spring-form pan

Directions

1. Preheat oven to 325° F.
2. Cool scalding milk, then whisk together with egg yolks.
3. Separately, measure and sift flour, sugar, salt and baking powder into a mixing bowl.
4. Make a well in the dry ingredients and add in the following order: the oil, vanilla, and the cooled egg yolk/milk mixture.
5. With mixer, beat until smooth.
6. Measure into a separate large bowl the egg whites and cream of tartar.
7. Whip until whites form very stiff peaks. Do not under beat!
8. Pour the batter gradually over the beaten egg whites, gently folding with a rubber spatula.
9. Pour into an ungreased 9-inch spring form pan and bake for 55 minutes; then increase temperature to 350° F and continue cooking for 10 to 15 minutes longer.
10. Cool and serve.

Desserts

Cherry Bars
Makes 12 servings

Ingredients

1	package spice or applesauce cake mix
2	eggs
1/3	cup water
6	Tablespoons butter or margarine
¾	cup dried apricots, chopped
3½	ounces coconut
½	cup maraschino cherries, chopped

Directions

1. Preheat oven to 350° F.
2. In a large mixing bowl, beat together cake mix, eggs, water and butter per cake mix directions.
3. Add apricots, coconut and cherries, stirring just until combined.
4. Spread evenly in greased 9 X 12 pan.
5. Bake for 18 to 20 minutes.
6. Cool in pan before cutting.

Carrot Cake
Makes 1 nine by twelve-inch cake; serves 12

Ingredients

2½	cups white flour
2	teaspoons baking soda
1	teaspoon cinnamon
½	teaspoon salt
½	cup sugar
1	cup oil
8	ounces crushed pineapple with juice
2	eggs
2	teaspoons vanilla extract
2	cups shredded carrots

Directions

1. Preheat oven to 350° F.
2. Mix sugar, oil, pineapple, eggs and vanilla and beat well.
3. Add remaining ingredients except carrots and blend well.
4. Stir in carrots.
5. Pour batter into a greased and floured 9 X 12 pan.
6. Bake for 30 to 40 minutes.

Flourless Chocolate Cake

Makes 8 servings

Ingredients

1	cup cocoa
6	eggs
1½	cups sugar
1	cup semi-sweet chocolate chips
1	cup butter
½	cup brandy
1½	cups pecan meal (or about 2 cups pecans ground fine in a food processor)

Additional chopped pecan pieces for garnish.
One nine-inch spring-form pan

Directions

1. Preheat oven to 325° F.
2. Melt butter in microwave, then stir in chocolate chips until smooth. If mixture does not continue to melt, return to microwave at 10 second intervals until fully melted. Set aside.
3. In separate bowl, mix cocoa, sugar and eggs on low, adding eggs one at a time. Increase speed as you add eggs, beating very well each time.
4. Fold together chocolate and egg mixtures, then fold in brandy and pecan meal.
5. Pour into 9-inch spring form pan lined with baking or parchment paper.
6. Bake at 325° F for about 50 minutes in a water bath (Bain-marie).
7. Run a knife around cake when done and place upside down on wire cooling rack.
8. Frost with a chocolate Ganache (see recipe on page 166). Press chopped pecans into the side of the cake but not on top.

Chef's tip

If you don't have a microwave, melt butter and chocolate chips in a Bain-marie, which is nothing more than a water bath. Place your container, (whether it's a pan, bowl, souffle dish, etc.) with food in a large shallow pan of warm water. This technique is designed to cook delicate dishes without breaking or curdling them.

Desserts

Pumpkin Roll
Makes 12 servings

Ingredients

Cake

3	eggs
1	cup sugar
2/3	cup pumpkin
¾	cup flour
1	teaspoon baking powder
2	teaspoons cinnamon
½	teaspoon salt
1	cup chopped pecans

Filling

1	cup powdered sugar
8	ounces cream cheese
4	Tablespoons butter
1	teaspoon vanilla

Directions

1. Preheat oven to 350° F.
2. Mix cake ingredients except pecans and pour into 11 x 15 pan lined with wax paper.
3. Sprinkle pecans over all.
4. Bake 15 minutes at 350° F.
5. Transfer onto a towel sprinkled with powdered sugar.
6. Roll up in towel.
7. Whip together filling ingredients until soft and fluffy.
8. When cool unroll carefully and fill with cheese mixture.
9. Re-roll and cool 1 hour.
10. Dust with powdered sugar and cut into individual circles for serving.

Strawberry Cake

Makes 8 to 10 servings

Ingredients

Cake

1	white cake mix
¾	cup vegetable oil
½	cup strawberries (fresh or frozen, drained well)
3	Tablespoons flour
4	eggs
1	package strawberry Jello, dissolved in ½ cup cold water

Two nine-inch cake pans, greased and floured

Frosting

1	stick butter or margarine, softened
1	box powdered sugar
½	cup drained frozen strawberries

Directions

1. Preheat oven to 325° F.
2. Mix all of the cake ingredients above together.
3. Pour into prepared cake pans.
4. Bake for 40 minutes.
5. Cool on racks.
6. Mix frosting ingredients and spread 1/3 on one cake, stack with second cake and spread top and sides with remaining frosting.

Nani's Blueberry Cupcakes

Makes 1 dozen

Ingredients

1¾	cups flour
½	cup sugar
2½	teaspoons baking powder
¾	teaspoon salt
1	egg, beaten
¾	cup milk
1/3	cup oil
1	cup blueberries

Directions

1. Preheat oven to 400° F.
2. Mix all ingredients except blueberries together until smooth.
3. Fold in blueberries, taking care not to crush.
4. Line muffin pan with paper or foil muffin cups.
5. Fill each cup half way full.
6. Bake for 25 minutes.

Desserts

Pavlova

Makes 6 four-inch meringue shells or one large Pavlova

Ingredients

3	egg whites, separated cold; bring to room temperature
1¼	cups superfine (castor) sugar
3	Tablespoons cold water
1	Tablespoon cornstarch
1	pinch salt
½	Tablespoon vanilla
1	Tablespoon white vinegar
½	cup white sugar

Chef's note

This light delicate crisp meringue cake with a soft sweet marshmallow center is said to have been invented in Australia and named in honor of the Russian ballerina, Anna Pavlova who toured the country in 1926.

Directions

1. Preheat to 200° F.
2. Beat egg whites in a very clean grease-free bowl until stiff.
3. Add water a little at a time.
4. Beat in sugar very slowly (if you can't find castor sugar, make your own by placing regular white sugar in a food processor until fine, 30-60 seconds.)
5. Mix cornstarch, salt, vanilla, and vinegar and fold in.
6. Put foil on a large cookie sheet and sprinkle with white sugar.
7. Using a food scoop, drop batter onto foil and make a small well in center.
8. Bake 4-inch shells for one hour. (Bake large Pavlova for 1 hour 30 minutes.)
9. Remove from oven, let cool to room temperature and top with whipped cream and fresh berries.

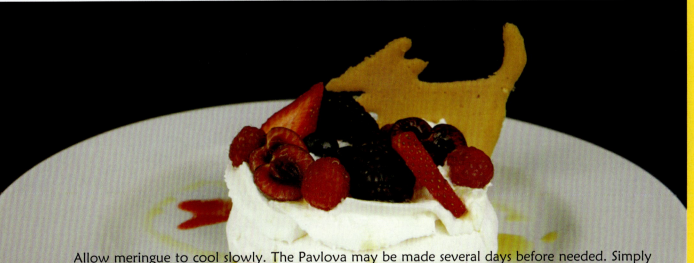

Allow meringue to cool slowly. The Pavlova may be made several days before needed. Simply store in a cool dry place in an airtight container. When ready to serve, make a soft whipped cream; spread on top of each Pavlova. Top with fresh fruit such as strawberries, raspberries, blueberries or passion fruit and kiwi. Drizzle top with fruit syrup and top with an additional dollo of whipped cream if desired.

Chocolate Self Saucing Pudding

Makes 8 servings

Ingredients

1 cup self rising flour
2 ounces butter
1 egg, beaten
2 teaspoons cocoa
½ cup castor sugar*
½ cup milk

Sauce

½ cup brown sugar
1¼ cups boiling water
1 Tablespoon cocoa powder

*To make castor sugar blend regular sugar in a blender.

Directions

1. Preheat oven to 350° F.
2. Sift flour and cocoa.
3. Cream butter and castor sugar, add eggs, mix well.
4. Stir in flour and milk alternately.
5. Pour into flameproof 6-cup casserole dish.

Sauce

6. Combine brown sugar and cocoa.
7. Sprinkle on top of mixture in casserole dish and pour boiling water gently on top.
8. Bake uncovered for 30 to 35 minutes.
9. Serve warm with whipped cream.

Chef's note

This is a favorite Australian dish I learned to make when I lived in Adelaide which is noted for its many festivals and sporting events, its food, wine and culture, and its long beach front. In South Australia, it is ranked highly as a livable city with wide boulevards and large public squares, and entirely surrounded by parklands.

Desserts

Nancy's Rice Pudding

Makes 6 servings

Ingredients

2/3	cup instant rice
2¾	cups milk
1/3	cup sugar
½	teaspoon salt
1/3	cup raisins
2	eggs, slightly beaten
1	teaspoon vanilla
¼	teaspoon ground nutmeg

Directions

1. Preheat oven to 375° F.
2. Mix the rice, milk, sugar, salt and raisins in a medium size saucepan.
3. Bring to a boil, stirring frequently.
4. Reduce the heat and simmer 10 minutes, stirring occasionally.
5. In a separate medium sized casserole dish, mix eggs, vanilla and nutmeg.
6. Slowly stir in the rice mixture.
7. Set dish in a pan of water.
8. Bake in center of oven for 20 to 30 minutes.
9. Cool for 1 hour.

Nancy's Sour Cream Cake

Makes 8 to 10 servings

Ingredients

Cake

½	pound butter (2 sticks)
3	cups sugar
½	pint sour cream
6	eggs
3	cups flour
½	teaspoon salt
1/8	teaspoon baking soda
2	teaspoons vanilla
1	Bundt pan, greased and floured

Glaze

½	stick butter
½	pound confectioners sugar
	orange or lemon juice

Directions

1. Preheat oven to 325° F.
2. Cream butter and sugar.
3. Add sour cream and eggs one at a time, stirring each into batter.
4. Sift flour, salt and baking soda and add to batter.
5. Add vanilla and stir mixture well.
6. Bake in Bundt pan for 1 hour and 15 minutes.
7. Turn cake onto plate.
8. Make glaze by mixing together butter and confectioners sugar until stiff.
9. Add orange or lemon juice until thin enough to pour over hot cake.

Desserts

Kathy's Sugar Cookies
Makes 3 dozen

Ingredients

1	cup butter or shortening
1½	cups sugar
3	eggs
1	teaspoon vanilla
3½	cups flour
2	teaspoons baking powder
1¼	teaspoons salt
	Turbinado, colored sugar or frosting for topping

Directions

1. Cream together butter or shortening, sugar, vanilla and eggs until light and fluffy.
2. Add dry ingredients and mix well. Cover and refrigerate at least 2 hours.
3. Preheat oven to 375º F. Lightly grease cookie sheet.
4. Divide dough in half.
5. Roll each half ¼ inch thick on lightly floured surface.
6. Cut into desired shapes with your favorite cookie cutters.
7. Leave plain for later frosting or sprinkle with turbinado or colored sugar so you don't need to frost after baking.
8. Place on cookie sheet.
9. Bake 7 to 8 minutes or until edges are light brown.
10. Remove from cookie sheet. Cool on wire rack.
11. May be iced with either recipe on page 166.
12. Add food coloring to frosting for the holidays.

Chef's note

This recipe was developed by my cousin Kathy Sheets-Retzloff who left this world far too early after a courageous fight against cancer.

Yellow Dog Cookies
Makes 24 cookies

Ingredients

1	stick butter, softened
3/4	cup powdered sugar, sifted
3	egg whites (use extra large eggs)
¾	cup flour plus 3 Tablespoons flour

Directions

1. Preheat oven to 325° F.
2. Cream butter and sifted powdered sugar together.
3. Add egg whites and whip with mixer until incorporated.
4. Fold in flour.
5. Drop by Tablespoon onto greased sheet.
6. Bake 5 to 7 minutes.
7. Remove immediately and roll around handle of wooden spoon or leave flat if desired.
8. After cooled, serve plain or dip into warm chocolate ganache (see recipe on page 166).

Chef's tip

At the Yellow Dog Cafe we use a stencil with dog shapes cut into it. We place a small amount of the batter on top of the stencil placed on a baking sheet, scraping the dough flat, leaving the imprint behind when you lift the stencil before baking. Try this with your favorite shapes.

Italian Wedding Cookies

Makes 40 cookies

Ingredients

- 1½ cups unsalted butter
- ¾ cup confectioners sugar
- ¼ teaspoon salt
- 1½ cups finely ground almonds or hazelnuts
- 2 teaspoons vanilla extract
- 3 cups sifted all purpose flour
- ½ cup confectioners sugar for rolling

Directions

1. Preheat oven to 325° F.
2. Cream butter in a bowl and gradually add confectioners sugar and salt
3. Beat until light and fluffy
4. Add almonds or hazelnuts and vanilla
5. Gradually add flour and mix well
6. Shape into balls using about 1 teaspoon for each cookie
7. Place on ungreased cookie sheet and bake 15 to 20 minutes. DO NOT BROWN.
8. Cool slightly, then roll in confectioners sugar.

Chocolate Peanut Butter Cookies

Makes 5 dozen

Ingredients

1	cup shortening
1	cup peanut butter
1	cup brown sugar
1	cup white sugar
2	eggs
2½	cups flour
1½	teaspoons baking soda
1	teaspoon baking powder
½	teaspoon salt
1	cup chocolate chips

Directions

1. Preheat oven to 375° F.
2. Blend shortening, peanut butter, sugars and eggs together in mixing bowl and beat until well blended.
3. Stir in flour, baking soda, baking powder and salt and blend well.
4. Fold in chocolate chips.
5. Drop dough by tablespoon onto cookie sheet. With floured fork, press tines into dough, then repeat at a 90 degree angle to make a crisscross pattern.
6. Bake 10 to 12 minutes.

Almond Crescents

Makes 4 dozen

Ingredients

1	cup butter
½	teaspoon almond extract
¾	cup sifted powdered sugar
2	cups all purpose flour
1	cup rolled oats, uncooked
½	cup finely chopped almonds

Powdered sugar for coating after baking.

Directions

1. Preheat oven to 325° F.
2. Whip butter and almond extract until fluffy.
3. Gradually blend in powdered sugar.
4. Add flour and mix well.
5. Stir in oats and almonds.
6. Shape dough into crescents.
7. Place on ungreased cookie sheet and bake 15 to 18 minutes or until light golden brown.
8. Sift powdered sugar over warm crescents.

Desserts

Oatmeal Cookies

Makes 4 dozen

Ingredients

- ½ cup butter
- ½ cup shortening
- 1 cup white sugar
- 1 cup light brown sugar
- 2 eggs
- 1 teaspoon vanilla extract
- 3 cups rolled oats
- 1 cup flour
- 1 teaspoon baking soda
- ½ teaspoon baking powder
- 1 teaspoon salt
- 1 teaspoon cinnamon
- 1 cup raisins
- 1 cup chopped walnuts

Directions

1. Preheat oven to 375° F.
2. Cream shortening, butter, and sugars together until smooth.
3. Stir in eggs and vanilla.
4. Combine dry ingredients and add to batter.
5. Mix until just combined.
6. Fold in raisins and walnuts.
7. Shape into 1½-inch balls and place two inches apart on ungreased cookie sheet.
8. Bake for 8 minutes or until done.

Nancy's Chocolate Cookies

Makes 4 dozen

Ingredients

2	eggs
1	cup sugar
¾	cup milk
¾	cup shortening
½	cup cocoa
1½	teaspoons baking soda
1½	teaspoons baking powder
1	teaspoon ground cloves
1	teaspoon cinnamon
1	teaspoon nutmeg
4	cups flour
1	pinch salt
½	cup raisins
½	cup walnuts, chopped
½	cup dried cherries or cranberries

Directions

1. Preheat oven to 400° F.
2. Melt and cool the shortening.
3. Add eggs, sugar and milk and blend together until light and fluffy.
4. Mix dry ingredients together and add to the egg mixture.
5. Blend well by hand or on low speed using a paddle, not a whisk attachment.
6. Once blended, stir in raisins, walnuts and cherries or cranberries.
7. Drop by spoon onto a greased cookie sheet.
8. Bake 10 to 12 minutes.
9. Allow to set for 1 minute before transferring cookies onto a cooling rack.

Desserts

Mia's Dutch Babies

Makes 4 to 6 servings

You'll need an 8-inch iron skillet and a blender.

Ingredients

- ¼ cup butter
- 4 eggs
- 1 cup milk
- 1 cup flour
- 2 Tablespoons honey
- 1 package frozen or fresh raspberries, strawberries, or fruit of choice, thawed (may also use pie filling)
- Whipped cream

Directions

1. Preheat oven to 425° F.
2. On top of stove, drop butter into an 8-inch black iron skillet and heat to medium high.
3. Meanwhile, in blender, whip eggs on high speed for one minute.
4. Gradually pour in milk through cap as you keep blending.
5. Add flour.
6. Blend for 30 seconds, then stop blending and scrape sides, blending any remaining flour into the mix.
7. Blend another 30 seconds or until batter is filled with air bubbles.
8. Immediately pour into skillet of bubbling hot butter.
9. Carefully slide in oven and bake for 25 minutes or until puffy and golden brown around tops.
10. Remove from oven and drizzle honey over entire dessert.
11. Cut Dutch Babies into 4 or 6 wedges and transfer to dessert plate.
12. Top with fruit and whipped cream.
13. Serve warm.

Potato Doughnut Balls

Makes 2 dozen

Ingredients

½	cup cold mashed potatoes
¾	cup sugar
½	stick butter
2	eggs
1½	cups un-sifted flour
2	teaspoons baking powder
½	teaspoon baking soda
½	teaspoon nutmeg
½	teaspoon cinnamon
¼	teaspoon vanilla
¼	teaspoon salt

Directions

1. Heat a heavy bottom pan with about 4 inches of oil to 340°F (if you don't have a deep fryer).
2. With electric mixer, mix all ingredients together.
3. Form 1-inch round balls.
4. Fry in small batches, making sure not to overload your pan.
5. Cook until golden brown.
6. Drain on paper towels.
7. Roll in powdered sugar and serve.

Desserts

CHURROS

Makes 2 dozen 4-inch churros
You will need a pastry bag and a large star tip.

Ingredients

1	cup water
2	Tablespoons light brown sugar
½	teaspoon salt
1/3	cup butter
1	cup all purpose flour
2	eggs
½	teaspoon vanilla extract
¼	cup sugar
½-1	teaspoon ground cinnamon, to taste
	Vegetable oil for frying

Directions

1. Preheat 2 inches of vegetable oil in a 10 or 12-inch heavy bottomed pot or deep fryer to 375° F.
2. In a separate dish mix ¼ cup sugar and cinnamon; set aside.
3. In a sauce pan, combine the water, brown sugar, salt and butter and bring to a boil.
4. Remove from heat and add flour, mixing well until completely blended.
5. In a separate bowl, combine eggs and vanilla and beat with a fork.
6. Add egg mixture to flour mixture and combine until well blended and all the egg is completely incorporated.
7. Fill your pastry bag with the churro dough and attach a large star tip.
8. Test the oil by squeezing out a small amount of dough into the hot oil. The dough should bubble up immediately.
9. Once the oil is hot enough, squeeze a 4-inch long section of dough into the oil. Take care not to burn yourself.
10. Once you have a perfect test churro, you may cook 4 to 6 churros at a time. Cook about one minute, then turn with a slotted spoon and cook an additional minute or until churros reach a nice golden brown color.
11. Drain on paper towels; while still warm, roll each churro in the sugar/cinnamon mixture until coated.
12. Serve warm.

Honey Crews

Homemade Dog Food

Let's not forget homemade treats for our canine friends. Here's a recipe we've used for years, a hearty healthy dish to welcome our furry friends.

Honey Pup Cakes

Makes 12 mini muffins

Ingredients

3/4 cup water
¼ cup applesauce, unsweetened
1 cup whole wheat flour
¼ cup chopped cooked chicken livers
1 teaspoon baking powder
1 egg, beaten slightly
1 Tablespoon honey

Directions

1. Preheat oven to 350° F.
2. Spray muffin tin with cooking spray.
3. Mix all wet ingredients thoroughly.
4. Combine dry ingredients in separate bowl.
5. Add wet to dry slowly, scraping well to make sure no dry mixture is left.
6. Pour into muffin tins.
7. Bake for 1 ¼ hours or until a toothpick inserted into center comes out dry.
8. Store in a sealed container.

Corn & Carrot Squares

Makes 16 servings

Ingredients

1	cup cornmeal
1	cup all-purpose flour
4	teaspoons baking powder
1	cup milk
1	egg, beaten
½	cup corn or canola oil
1	small can corn
1	small can diced carrots

Directions

1. Preheat oven to 425° F.
2. Combine dry ingredients.
3. Add liquids and beat until smooth.
4. Drain liquid from canned vegetables, then fold corn and carrots into batter.
5. Pour into a greased, 8-inch square baking pan.
6. Bake 15 to 20 minutes.
7. When cooled, cut into sixteen 2-inch squares.

Cindy and Arlo Finch, Spring 2005

Reba Jane & Dixie Mae Sullivan

Chicken and Rice Entree

Makes 3 cups

Ingredients

- 1¾ cup white rice
- 2½ cups water
- 1 chicken bouillon
- 2 chicken breasts, cooked and diced
- 2 eggs, beaten
- 1 Tablespoon canola oil

Directions

1. Boil water with bouillon cube.
2. Add rice and turn temperature down to low; simmer for 20 minutes or until liquid is completely absorbed.
3. Add chicken to rice and bring to room temperature.
4. In frying pan, bring oil to medium heat.
5. Add rice and chicken and stir until mixed, about 1 minute.
6. Pour eggs over rice and chicken.
7. Stir until egg is completely cooked.
8. Store in refrigerator until ready to feed your favorite pooch.
9. Microwave entree for 30 seconds or until chill dissipates.
10. Serve.

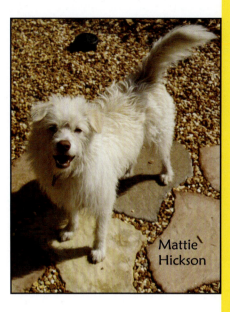

Mattie Hickson

Blanche

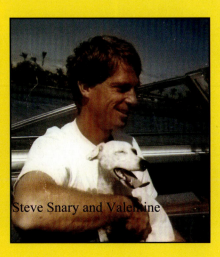

Steve Snary and Valentine

Dusty and Teddy Crews

WE LOVE CATS, TOO!

Nancy and Stuart are proud owners of a beautiful black cat named Winston, who they consider part of the Yellow Dog family. Below are some favorite photos of beautiful felines.

Glossary of Cooking Terms

al: Italian meaning "at the," "to the" or "on the." Example, al dente means "to the tooth", describing pasta or other food cooked until it offers a slight resistance when bitten into. Al dente signifies not to overcook a particular food.

à la: French for "in the manner of." It is short for "à la mode de" signifying a style of preparation. In America, this term refers to pie topped with ice cream.

à la carte: a French term meaning that each item on the menu is priced separately.

al fresco: Italian for "fresh" or "cook," usually referring to dining outdoors.

amaretto: a liqueur with the flavor of almonds, although it is often made with apricot pit kernels.

anchovy: small silvery fish that comes from the Mediterranean and southern European coastlines. These fish are filleted, salt cured and canned in oil.

anchovy paste: a combination of anchovies, vinegar, spices and water that comes in tubes and used on canapés or for flavoring.

andouille: a spicy, smoked sausage used in Cajun food such as jambalaya and gumbo. Originally from France, andouille is great served cold as an hors d'oeuvre.

anise: a spice related to parsley. The leaves and seed have a distinctive, sweet licorice flavor used to enhance cookies, cakes and savory dishes. Anise is also used to flavor drinks like anisette and ouzo.

appetizer: any small, bite-sized food served before a meal; used synonymously with the French term *hors d'oeuvre*, which normally refers to finger food. The term *appetizers* applies to a first course served at the table.

arroz: Spanish for rice.

arugula: a somewhat bitter aromatic salad green with a peppery mustard flavor.

au jus: French for meat served with its own natural juices, such as beef au jus.

au lait: French for "with milk." It refers to food or beverages served or prepared with milk.

baba: a rich, light currant or raisin-studded yeast cake soaked in rum or kirsch syrup.

baba ghanoush or ghanouj: a Middle Eastern puree of eggplant, tahini, olive oil, lemon juice and garlic used as a spread or dip for pita or flat bread.

baguette: French bread formed into a long, narrow cylindrical loaf with a brown crust and light, chewy interior.

bain-marie: a French term meaning to cook food gently; water bath

baked blind: referring to a pastry shell before it is filled. The shell is pricked all over with a fork and weighted down to prevent it from blistering and rising.

baking soda: sodium bicarbonate; an alkali used as leavening in baked goods. Baking soda releases carbon dioxide gas bubbles when combined with acidic ingredients such as yogurt, buttermilk or molasses, causing the batter to rise. Batter with baking soda should be placed in the oven immediately.

bananas Foster: bananas Foster is Brennan's of New Orleans, Louisiana, signature dessert created by Paul Blange in 1951 in honor of Richard Foster, Brennan's friend and New Orleans' Crime Commissioner at the time. It consists of sliced bananas, butter, sugar, cinnamon, banana liqueur, and flaming rum served over ice cream.

baste: to spoon or brush food as it cooks with melted butter, meat drippings or a liquid.

béarnaise: a classic French sauce made with a reduction of vinegar, wine, tarragon and shallots, finished with egg yolks and butter and served with meat, fish, eggs or vegetables.

béchamel: a basic French white sauce made by stirring milk into a butter-flour roux, named after its inventor Louis XIV's steward Louis de Béchamel.

beurre: French for "butter."

bisque: a thick, rich soup usually consisting of puréed seafood or a vegetable and cream.

blackened: a cooking technique whereby meat or fish rubbed with a Cajun spice mixture is cooked in a cast iron skilled that is heated until almost red hot.

blanc: French for "white," such as beurre blanc or "white butter."

blanch: plunging vegetables or fruit into boiling water quickly, then into cold water to stop the cooking process.

blini: small thin yeast raised pancakes typically served with sour cream and caviar or smoked salmon; originated in Russia.

boil: heating a liquid to 212 ° F. A full rolling boil is one that cannot be dissipated by stirring.

brochette: French for "skewer."

brûlée: French for "burned," referring to creme brûlée, burnt cream or custard.

bruschetta: a garlic bread made by rubbing slices of toasted bread with garlic cloves, drizzling it with olive oil, salted and peppered, then heated under a broiler.

canapé: small pieces of toasted or un-toasted bread topped with a garnish and served as an appetizer; French for "couch."

caper: a small flower bud of a bush native to the Mediterranean and parts of Asia where they are picked, sun dried and pickled in a vinegar brine.

caramelize: burnt sugar made by heating sugar until it liquefies and becomes a clear syrup; sugar may also be caramelized by sprinkling on top of food and heated in the broiler or with a torch until the sugar melts and becomes crispy.

cayenne pepper: a hot pungent powder made from various tropical chilies, also called red pepper.

Glossary

chipotle: dried jalapeño chili pepper.

chop suey: a Chinese-American dish that includes small pieces of meat or shrimp, mushrooms, bean sprouts, water chestnuts, bamboo shoots and onions cooked together and served over rice.

churro: a Spanish and Mexican sweet-dough spiral that is deep-fried and eaten like a doughnut covered with cinnamon and sugar.

chutney: a spicy condiment containing fruit, vinegar, sugar and spices, with a texture ranging from chunky to smooth.

cilantro: the bright green leaves and stems of the coriander plant.

clarify: to clear a cloudy liquid by removing any sediment; butter may be clarified by adding hot water and boiling for about 15 minutes, then strained through several layers of cheesecloth and chilled, after which the top layer of fat should be clear of residue.

concassé: French for crush or grind; rough chop.

conch: a gastropod mollusk encased in a brightly colored spiral shell found in southern waters.

créme brûlée: French for "burnt cream." A chilled custard topped with sugar which is then caramelized with a torch, making the topping brittle.

créme fraîche: a mixture of 1 cup whipping cream and 2 tablespoons buttermilk in a covered glass container and left at room temperature from 8 to 24 hours until very thick; it can be boiled without curdling and is delicious spooned over fresh fruit or other desserts like warm cobblers or puddings.

cremino: a common brown mushroom; the portobello mushroom is a fully matured cremino.

crostini: little toasts.

crouton: a cube of bread that has been browned by baking.

curry powder: a pulverized blend of spices, herbs and seeds such as cardamom, chilies, cinnamon, cloves, coriander, cumin, fennel seed, mace, nutmeg, pepper, and turmeric widely used in Indian dishes.

date: a fruit that grows in clusters on the giant date palm, native to the Middle East; dates may be eaten fresh or dried.

deglaze: a cooking technique for removing and dissolving caramelized bits of food from a pan in order to make a pan sauce; stirring to loosen browned bits of food on the bottom, used as a base for a sauce to be served on the sautéed food.

degrease: refers to the process of removing fat from the surface of a sauce, soup, stew or broth.

dollop: a small glob of soft food such as whipped cream or mashed potato; refers to casually adding an ingredient without measuring, such as a dollop of sour cream.

Dutch oven: a large pot or kettle, usually made of cast iron with a tight fitting lid, used for moist cooking methods such as braising and stewing; may be used on top of stove or in oven.

entrée: in the United States, it is the main course of a meal; in parts of Europe, it refers to the dish served between the fish and meat courses; in Australia, the entrée is the first course or appetizer.

fillet: a boneless piece of meat or fish; or the process of removing the bones from meat or fish.

Florentine, a la: refers to dishes, usually eggs or fish that are presented on a bed of spinach and topped with mornay sauce and sometimes sprinkled with cheese and browned lightly in the oven.

focaccia: an Italian bread shaped into a large flat round liberally brushed or drizzled with olive oil and sprinkled with salt.

french, to: to cut a vegetable or meat lengthwise into very thin strips; or to cut the meat away from the end of a rib or chop to expose the bone.

frittata: an Italian omelet that usually has the ingredients mixed in with the eggs rather than being folded inside. A frittata can be flipped or finished in the oven.

escargot: French for snail.

ganache: a rich icing or filling made of semisweet chocolate and whipping cream by heating and stirring the ingredients together until the chocolate has melted.

garam masala: a favorite blend of ground spices used by Indian cooks; the spices can include black pepper, cinnamon, cloves, coriander, cumin, cardamom, dried chilies, fennel, mace, nutmeg and others.

Hoisin sauce: a sweet spicy sauce made from soybean paste and flavored with garlic, sugar, chilies, and other spices. Hoisin sauce is a favorite dipping sauce and is the main ingredient in many Chinese barbecue recipes. It may also be used to glaze meat or duck.

gazpacho: a cold uncooked soup usually made from a puréed mix of fresh tomatoes, sweet bell peppers, onions, celery, cucumber, garlic, olive oil and vinegar.

gnocchi: Italian for "dumplings" made from potatoes, flour or farina.

grits: any coarsely ground grain such as corn, oats or rice; most often refers to "Hominy" grits which are dried white or yellow corn kernels with the hull and germ removed; grits are served as a side dish or part of a casserole.

guacamole: a Mexican specialty of mashed avocado and various seasonings and used as a dip, sauce or topping.

hollandaise: a creamy sauce made with butter, egg yolks and lemon juice, used over vegetables, fish and egg dishes.

hors d'oeuvre: small appetizers served before a meal.

Glossary

hummus: a thick Middle Eastern mixture made from mashed chickpeas seasoned with lemon juice, garlic and olive oil, served as a dip or sauce.

jalapeño chile: smooth dark green chilies that turn scarlet red when ripened, ranging from hot to very hot, available fresh and canned; in their dried form they are called chipotles.

jicama: a large bulbous root vegetable with a thin brown white skin and white crunch flesh with a sweet nutty flavor; good raw and cooked, it hails from Mexico and South America. It is also called Mexican potato and jam bean root.

Julienne: foods that are cut into thin matchstick strips, often used as a garnish. Julienne also means "to cut food into very thin strips."

roux: a mixture of flour and fat that, after being slowly cooked over low heat, is used to thicken mixtures such as soups and sauces. White Roux is made with butter and cooked until it begins to turn beige. Blond Roux is made with butter and cooked until it turns a pale gold. Brown Roux can be made from butter, meat drippings or pork/beef fat and cooked to a deep golden brown.

kebab; kabob: small chunks of meat, fish, shellfish or vegetables usually marinated before threaded on a skewer and grilled over coals.

Kiwi: a fruit that looks like the large brown egg of the kiwi bird from New Zealand; the inside contains a beautiful brilliant green flesh dotted with tiny edible black seeds. Kiwi fruit is grown in New Zealand and California.

knead: mixing and working a dough to form it into a network of gluten strands that stretches and expands, allowing it to hold in the gas bubbles formed by a leavener like yeast which allows the dough to rise.

kosher: food that conforms to strict Jewish biblical laws, prepared under the supervision of a rabbi, and resulting in a "pure" food with an inherent hallmark of wholesomeness and quality.

mandoline: a small hand-operated slicer with adjustable blades for thin to thick slicing and for julienne and french fry cutting.

Marsala: a Sicilian wine with a rich smoky flavor derived from oxidation during aging; may be served as an aperitif or used in cooking.

masala: an Indian word for a spice blend using cardamom, coriander and mace or a more complex blend of 10 or more spices depending on the cook.

mayonnaise: a thick, creamy dressing made of vegetable oil, egg yolks, lemon juice or vinegar and seasoning; all mayonnaise should be refrigerated once made or opened.

mince: to cut food into tiny pieces.

mornay sauce: a béchamel sauce with Parmesan and Swiss cheese added; can be varied by adding fish or chicken stock or cream or egg yolks.

panko: Japanese breadcrumbs used to coat fried foods; these breadcrumbs are coarser than normal to create a crunchy crust.

paté: French for "pie," it generally refers to a variety of well-seasoned ground meat preparations that vary from satiny smooth and spreadable to ground and chunky.

Pavlova: a famous Australian dessert made with a meringue base topped with whipped cram and fruit; it was named after the Russian ballerina Anna Pavlova when she visited Australia.

pecorino: a hard aged cheese made from sheep's milk.

pesto: Italian for "pounded;" an uncooked sauce made from pine nuts, garlic, fresh basil, parmesan or pecorino cheese and olive oil and often served with pasta.

phyllo: Greek for "leaf," referring to tissue-thin layers of pastry dough used in a variety of Greek and Near Eastern sweet desserts such as baklava; also spelled *filo*, it comes packaged fresh and frozen in most supermarkets.

poach: to cook food gently in liquid just below the boiling point.

ponzu: a Japanese dipping sauce most often made with lemon juice or rice vinegar, soy sauce, mirin, sake, seaweed and dried bonito flakes.

portobello mushroom: an extremely large, dark brown mushroom that is the fully mature form of the crimino mushroom.

proof: to dissolve yeast in a warm liquid often combined with a small amount of sugar, then set aside in a warm place for 5 to 10 minutes until it becomes bubbly, proving that the yeast is active; *proof* is also a term used to indicate the amount of alcohol in liquor.

ramekin: a small individual baking dish resembling a miniature souffle dish; the word also refers to a tiny baked pastry filled with a creamy cheese custard.

reconstitute: to return a dehydrated food such as dried mushrooms to its original state by adding a liquid, usually water.

reduce: to boil a liquid or sauce rapidly until the volume is reduced by evaporation, thickening and intensifying the flavor of the ingredient which is now called a *reduction*.

render: to melt animal fat such as bacon over low heat which separates it from any tissue and turns it brown and crisp, resulting in a clear fat that is then strained through a paper filter or fine cheesecloth to remove the residue which is often referred to as *cracklings*.

rice paper: an edible translucent dough made from water combined with the pith of an Asian shrub called the rice-paper plant; used to wrap foods to be eaten as is or deep-fried.

salamander: a kitchen tool used to brown or caramelize the top layer of food, such as sugar, leaving the inside layer cool; a type of broiler.

Glossary

salsa: Mexican and Spanish for "sauce," which can be cooked or made of fresh mixtures of ingredients such as tomatoes, green chilies and cilantro and used for dipping.

sambal: a condiment made of a blend of chilies, brown sugar, salt, garlic, onion and even tamarind concentrate or coconut milk, usually accompanying rice and curried dishes, popular throughout Indonesia, Malaysia and southern India.

sauté: to cook quickly in a small amount of oil in a skillet; to fry.

seviche: a popular Latin appetizer of raw fish marinated in citrus juice, usually lime.

slurry: a thin paste of water and flour or cornstarch which is then stirred into a hot soup, stew or sauce as a thickener.

soufflé: a light airy mixture of an egg yolk based sauce or puree to which stiffly beaten egg whites are added; baked soufflés are fragile, as the trapped hot air escapes, causing the soufflé to deflate; chilled dessert soufflés are not as fragile.

tamarind: the fruit of the Indian date which has a sour-sweet pulp used to season East Indian and Middle Eastern cuisines much like lemon juice is used in Western culture. It is an integral ingredient in Worcestershire sauce.

tapenade: a thick paste made from capers, anchovies, ripe olives, olive oil, lemon juice and other seasonings.

turbinado: raw sugar that has been steam cleaned; coarse turbinado crystals are blond colored and have a delicate molasses flavor.

vol-au-vent: a puff pastry shell resembling a pot with a lid and classically filled with a cream sauce based mixture, usually of chicken, fish, meat or vegetables.

wasabi: Japanese horseradish available as a paste or a powder, making a green-colored condiment with a sharp fiery flavor.

Worcestershire sauce: a sauce first bottled in Worcester, England, it is thin, dark and piquant and used to season meats, gravies, and soups. The ingredients usually include garlic, soy sauce, tamarind, onions, molasses, lime, anchovies, and vinegar.

zest: the outermost skin layer of citrus fruit removed using a citrus zester, paring knife or vegetable peeler, leaving the white pith behind.

WEIGHTS & MEASURES

1 Tablespoon (Tbsp) = 3 teaspoons (tsp) = 14 grams

1/4 cup = 4 Tablespoons = 56.7 grams

1/3 cup = 5 Tablespoons + 1 teaspoon = 75.6 grams

3/8 cup = 6 Tablespoons

1/2 cup = 8 Tablespoons = 113 grams

2/3 cup = 10 Tablespoons + 2 teaspoons

3/4 cup = 12 Tablespoons

8 fluid ounces (fl oz) = 1 cup = 237 ml

1 pint (pt) = 2 cups = 474 ml

1 quart (qt) = 2 pints = .964 liters

4 cups = 1 quart

1 gallon (gal) = 4 quarts = 16 cups

16 ounces (oz) = 1 pound (lb)

1 milliliter (ml) = 1 cubic centimeter (cc)

100 ml = 3.4 fluid oz

1 kilogram = 2.205 pounds = 35 ounces

237 ml = 1 cup

1 liter = 34 fluid oz = 4.2 cups = 2.1 pints = 1.06 quarts = 0.26 gallon

Relax at...

Escape to...

Bring A Friend to...

Howl at the moon at...

212

Laugh it up at...

High tail it to the...

Enjoy the artwork and dog memorabilia that are so much a part of life at Yellow Dog Cafe!

Index

A
acknowledgements	4

B
bain-marie	183
batter	
crepes	55
pancake	56
tempura	53
waffle	56
Yellow Dog dry fry	54
Yellow Dog fry	54
beef	
golumpki	141
meatloaf	144
pineapple skewers	117
shepherds pie	139
short ribs	138
with broccoli	145
beignet	49
biscuits	48
Borton, Nancy Tinio	12
Borton, Stuart	10
bread	
biscuits	48
Bistro cinnamon rolls	45
cheese	48
focaccia	50
Italian	51
potato rolls	44
pudding	162
soft rolls	49
sticky buns	46
zucchini	51
brownies	158

C
cake	
carrot	182
cheesecake	159
chiffon	181
chocolate	165
flourless chocolate	183
Mississippi mud	164
New Zealand kiwi cheese	179
Pavlova	186
pumpkin roll	184
sour cream	189
strawberry	185
caprese	114
cats	203
ceviche	
pineapple	119
cheesecake	
lobster	113
s'mores	156
chicken	
onion crusted with caramel citrus glaze	151
piccata	149
churros	198
chutney	
tamarind orange	124
walnut	40
cookies	
almond crescents	193
cherry bar	182
chocolate	195
chocolate peanut butter	193
Italian wedding	192
oatmeal	194
orange crisps	180
peanut butter oatmeal	170
sugar	190
Yellow Dog	191
cooking terms	204
corn fritters	54
crab	
cakes	123
spicy dip	123
creme brulee	161
crepes	
apple cinnamon	160
batter	55
chicken	116
crostini	
goat cheese	129
crust	
butter	168

graham cracker	167
never fail	168
cupcakes	
blueberry	185

D

dates	
stuffed	126
dip	
crab	123
dog food	200
chicken & rice entree	202
corn & carrot squares	201
honey pup cakes	200
dough	
basic for meat pies	47
Nancy's pizza	52
doughnuts	
Churros	198
potato	197
Dutch babies	196

E

eggs	
Jason	60
Benedict	59
crab vol-au-vent	62
florentine omelette	64
frittata	66
lobster omelette	65
poached	59
quiche	63
sardou	60
shrimp frittata	67
spinach frittata	68

F

Falls Mill	70
frittata	
shrimp	67
frosting	
butter	166
chocolate ganache	166
creamy	166

G

glaze	
lime and ginger	41
caramel citrus	151
glossary	204
gnocchi	147
gołumpki	141
gravy	
pork	30
sausage	30
grits	
aloha	71
basic from Falls Mill	70
cheese	71
Florida shrimp	72
jalapeno	71
guacamole	96

H

hamburger	
stuffed	98
Hollandaise	40
Creole	60
hummus	129

L

labanee	133
lamb	
lolly pops	115
skewers	116
lobster	
cheesecake	113

M

marmalade	
red onion	39
marshmallows	157
mayonnaise	41
meat pie	133
Aussie beef pastries	132

meatballs	
rosemary skewered	126
muffins	
basic	163

O

omelette	
Florentine	64

P

panzarotti	
leek and mushroom	118
pie	
banana cream	177
butterscotch	175
chocolate cream	178
coconut	171
coconut cream	174
Jill Jone's real pumpkin	172
Key lime	173
lemon meringue	176
meat	133
peanut butter	170
peanut butter custard	169
pecan	175
potato and meat	134
spinach	134
pie crust	
butter	168
plantain chips	117
polenta	
with spicy shrimp ragu	122
pork	
brochettes	127
chops with Tabasco molasses	142
medallions with shrimp	143
stuffed chops	150
with shrimp and bok choy	146
potatoes	
pommes Anna	102
products	20
pudding	
bread	162
chocolate self saucing	187
rice	188
pumpkin	
roll	184

R

red pepper	
roasted roll	125
rice	
cilantro	100
wild	101
blini	131
wild vegetable griddle cakes	101
roux	29

S

salad	
blueberry spinach	89
coleslaw	88
copper penny	90
jicama	82
macaroni	87
potato	87
tropical macaroni	86
salsa	42
black bean and mango	42
salmon	152
sandwiches	
California dreamer	96
good ole dog	95
lady dog	93
shrimp salad	97
stuffed hamburger	98
tuna (Top Dog)	92
Yellow Dog favorite	94
sauces	
amaretto	37
barbecue	37
beurre blanc	40
cheese	32
cherry pepper	33
hollandaise	40
lime and ginger glaze	41
lobster	36
malted mint	35
mushroom	31

pesto		36
ponzu		32
raspberry		38
remoulade		39
roasted red pepper		35
saffron cream		32
sambal dipping		34
satay		33
spring roll dipping		33
sriracha		124
whiskey		162
white		31
scallop		
mousse		125
shrimp		
bacon brochettes		128
Louisiana		148
mousse		125
spicy grilled		124
spicy ragu		122
with pork & bok choy		146
with pork medallions		143
Vietnamese spring roll		130
sides		
chayote succotash		107
cilantro rice		100
Delmonico potatoes		108
fried onions		105
potato cakes		106
potato puffs		106
spinach souffle		103
stuffing		104
wild rice		101
wild rice vegetable griddle cakes		101
soup		
black bean		81
caldo gallego		83
chicken velvet		74
cream of mushroom		78
cream of tomato		75
Manhattan chowder		80
onion		77
pumpkin		84
strawberry gazpacho		82
vegetable bean		76
spice mix		
beef		26
blackening		28
chili		26
creole		27
garam masala		28
house		26
lamb rub		27
pork		27
Louisiana seasoning		148
spreads		
rocket mayo		41
syrup		
simple		38

T

tahina		129
tapanade		
olive		120
toast		120
tarts		
zucchini, pear & cheese		132
topping		
crumb		167
tuna		
pistachio crusted skewers		112
sesame crusted		140
tuna tataki		109

V

vegetarian		
eggplant stew		81
Lady Dog sandwich		93
pie		133
spinach pie		134
spicy sesame vegetables		121

W

weights and measures		211